Unshattered

OVERCOMING TRAGEDY AND CHOOSING A BEAUTIFUL LIFE

Carol J. Decker
with Stacey L. Nash

SHADOW
MOUNTAIN

TO MY TALENTED BIG BROTHER SHAWN,
who I miss every day.

Thank you for teaching me to be fearless,
for always making me laugh,
and for showing me what true compassion
and friendship look like.

I love you so much, and I know you're
always with me in my heart.

—CJD

Photo on page 2 courtesy of Willow Eskridge.
Photos on pages 181 and 184 courtesy of Coral von Zumwalt.
All other photos courtesy of the author.

© 2018 Carol Decker and Stacey L. Nash

Visit us at ShadowMountain.com

Library of Congress Cataloging-in-Publication Data

Names: Decker, Carol J., 1975– author. | Nash, Stacey L., 1980– author.
Title: Unshattered : overcoming tragedy and choosing a beautiful life / Carol J. Decker and Stacey Nash.
Description: Salt Lake City, Utah : Shadow Mountain, [2018] | Includes bibliographical references.
Identifiers: LCCN 2017055090 | ISBN 9781629724164 (paperbound)
Subjects: LCSH: Decker, Carol J., 1975– | Women amputees—Biography. |Blind—Biography. | LCGFT: Autobiographies.
Classification: LCC RD796.A2 D43 2018 | DDC 617.5/8092 [B]—dc23
LC record available at https://lccn.loc.gov/2017055090

Printed in the United States of America
Edwards Brothers Malloy, Ann Arbor, MI

10 9 8 7 6 5 4 3 2 1

Contents

Introduction

by Scott C. Decker, DMD

Carol and I met at what was then Ricks College in 1995, during our sophomore year. After dating for three years, we married in March of 1998. We moved to Seattle so I could manage a warehouse full time while going to school at the University of Washington. While living in Seattle, Carol worked as a medical assistant at multiple cardiology offices. She became well known for being a hard worker, a good friend, and a kind person. Carol has always had a knack for making friends. People are just attracted to her.

After I finished my studies at the University of Washington, we moved to Boston so I could go to dental school full time. Carol worked more than full time to support us while I was in school. She again made many friends and gained the trust of her colleagues at the endocrinologist's office where she worked.

Scott and me, growing stronger as we manage trials together.

Leaving Boston was harder for her than for me because of all the friends she'd made.

After I graduated in 2005, we moved back to Seattle. We lived close to Carol's new job in Seattle at another cardiology office, and I commuted for two years as an associate dentist in Tacoma. In 2006, we decided to start a family, and on New Year's Eve, our first daughter, Chloe, was born. In late 2007, we found out Carol was pregnant with our second child, Safiya.

This book is about Safiya's birth, how it changed our family forever, and how the strongest woman you could ever know fought to be part of our lives.

In June 2008, Carol was put into early labor with an infection that developed into sepsis. It almost killed her. That infection led to some physical disabilities that she—that *we*—have had to learn to live with and eventually try to thrive with.

Early in Carol's illness, I was at the hospital all the time and balancing a new dental practice and two kids. We had an amazing support system from both of our families. We could not have gotten to this point without them. During the second hospitalization, I found it much harder to be with Carol during all of the plastic surgeries due to my work and family obligations. I am forever grateful to my brother-in-law, Heath, who has given our family more service and care than anyone. I might not have gotten through those months if he hadn't been at Carol's bedside when I couldn't be.

Throughout the hospitalizations, Carol's return home, and even now, to a lesser degree, I have tried to search for what would make her life easier. I have constantly worked to make sure we have the proper insurance coverage to afford the technology she needs to thrive.

When Carol got home from the hospital, I thought there had to be a book out there that explained how to deal with everything before us. I soon had to learn that every step Carol took would be at her pace and would require tools specific to her. At first, we relied on what was easiest. Sometimes we tried things that didn't work. When she first came home, I would carry her around a lot. I did that off and on for the first couple of years as she went through additional surgeries. But over time that wasn't necessary. For a few years, she could only wear her prosthetic legs so long before she got exhausted and had to take them off. Slowly, that went away, and she could wear them all day. We used to take her wheelchair along if we went somewhere so she could get off of her legs, but that need has gone away as well.

Slowly, Carol began to pick a goal and master it if she could (a habit she's continued to this day). In that sense, she was no different than she was before sepsis. For a couple of years I did her makeup for her, but eventually she made a goal to do it herself. Before long, I didn't need to do that anymore. I used to email and text for her, but she can do that for herself now. We grocery shop in a way that allows Carol to eat at the house by herself. I guess the moral is that she, and we, her family, have tried to work hard and have had to learn that even though there isn't a book on how we should do this, we can slowly figure it out simply by living.

Our daughters and I have to do a bit more than the average family. I am the cook now, something I never was before Carol's infection. Our daughters are very responsible and help out in every way they can. We used to all go into public bathrooms together, but now the girls help their mother if needed. Carol can do it herself, but it is easier if someone can direct her. We used to help Carol pick out clothes, but she does that herself now, too. We just give her the yea or nay on some outfits, usually when she has to dress up. We still haven't mastered how she can safely use the oven and stove by herself. We have tried, with some small success, but there's still a long way to go.

As I've gone to some of Carol's speaking engagements, more and more people have asked how we have done this for the last decade. The first thing that always comes to mind is our extended family and a strong support system. Everyone in our town knows and accepts us.

I struggled a lot on a personal level with what happened to us, especially in the first couple years. It was like being married to a totally new person, and it was hard. During the early years, I went through the day-to-day motions. There wasn't a lot of time to think about much else besides working and taking care of Carol and the girls. I eventually got to a point where I didn't want as much outside help to make our family run. I had to decide to make some positive changes in my own life so I could do what it took to make my family run smoothly with just Carol and me.

Around that time, I remember someone asking me why I stayed with Carol. My immediate thought was because it was the right thing to do. But then I realized, I hadn't thought and couldn't think of living my life with anyone else. When you find your soul mate, you find your soul mate. Carol and I have had many ups and downs over these last nine years, but our marriage is in a great place. Like the rest of our goals, it has taken love, hard work, and help as it continues to evolve.

I am so proud of Carol and all that she accomplishes. I'm proud to be part of her successes, but even prouder of the success she has found that has had nothing to do with me.

CHAPTER 1

Resilient

"There will be key moments for you that may change the course of your life in an instant."
—*Gérald Caussé*

Chalk dust floated through the air as the smell of plastic mats and sweat filled the gymnasium. I tightened every muscle in my eleven-year-old body, fixing my eyes on the gritty beam beneath my feet.

Balance.

Confidence.

Courage.

The beat of my heart pounded the words into my head like an echoing drum.

I heard my dad's voice in the crowd. Concentration kept his cheers from sinking in, but my heart grew stronger knowing he was there.

Eyes fixed on the beam, solid and steady, I jumped, tucking legs to chest. I landed without a sound, the beam still

*Me (center) in seventh grade with two friends, Amy (left)
and Lisa (right), from my gymnastics team.*

firmly beneath me. With feet perfectly placed and my core
pulled taut, a smile tugged at the corners of my mouth. Had I
been on the playground with friends, I would have burst into
laughter that would have drawn everyone near me into fits of
uncontrollable giggles. I resisted the urge. This wasn't the time
for a lapse in focus—not in the midst of a competition. My
love of the challenge was too great.

All that mattered in that moment was my next move, a
complex series of turns. I'd spent weeks perfecting it and knew
I was nailing the routine. With my arms overhead, I took a
steadying breath before I hardened my core muscles, brought
my arms around, and started the turn that would take me
through to my dismount. I hadn't gotten to the tuck before I
knew something was wrong.

Somewhere between the beam and the mat, the gym
churned through my vision as I felt the rough, sandpaper-like
surface of the beam tear down the inside of my knee and thigh.

I didn't have time to consider that up was down before my foot hit the mat, quickly followed by the rest of me.

Stunned by the fall and confused by the burning in my leg, I stared at my feet. How could this have happened? It wasn't as though I had never fallen in competition before, but not at this point in my beam routine. I knew it too well, had practiced too hard.

I could have stood up, put my arms over my head, and signaled to the judges that I was done, losing a significant portion of my points. I could have walked away, forfeiting all of my points and letting down my team. I could have quit gymnastics altogether, tired of scraping my legs, landing on my neck, and trying to push through the fear of trying a new element. Essentially, I had to give up or pick up.

Though a small part of me wanted to quit, the better, stronger part refused to stay sitting on the mat. I don't remember standing up, but suddenly I was back on two feet with my hands on the beam, taking a deep breath.

Fear coiled itself around my fluttering stomach. What if I fell again?

This time my dad's "You can do it!" came through loud and clear. My sidelong glance revealed my parents' faces, concerned and encouraging. My two brothers sat silently next to them, their bodies leaning forward as though they were trying to will me back onto the beam.

I couldn't let them down—them or my coach or my teammates. And last of all, I couldn't disappoint myself.

With hands firmly set, I hoisted myself back on the beam, ignoring the pricks of pain as I slid past the burning scrapes on my leg. Hesitation marked the first bend of my knee to hit the pose that should have followed the tuck. The slight shake of my leg enlarged the bubble of fear that was trying to swell its way into life. I quickly popped it by focusing on moving my body with the precision my coach expected every time I entered the gym.

Each step, bend, leap, and turn brought more confidence until I was ready for the dismount. I took a brief check of my body position.

With as much power and force as my small body could create, I jumped and twisted in a blur until my feet hit the mat—knees bent, muscles stretched, leg burning. I refused to take a step to check my balance. After my fall, I wouldn't let the landing get away from me. When I was sure I had it, I raised my arms overhead with a forced grin covering my face.

My parents' whistles and claps somehow reached my ears over the shouts of my teammates and coach.

There was no excited bouncing off the mat into the open arms of my coach like usual. But there wasn't a lecture, either. I didn't need it. I was harder on myself than my coach could ever be, and he knew it. My confidence and young pride had taken a hit. We'd be lucky to finish in the top three with that performance.

I couldn't look my teammates in the eyes, but I felt one sit next to me as I got ready to move to the next event. Her name escapes me now. I remember not wanting to see the disappointment or pity on her face. Without a word and with nothing more than a light touch on my arm, she expressed her sympathy before moving on. I appreciated her quiet support.

Then it hit me—vault was next!

It wasn't my favorite, but I'd learned to take the good (floor routine) with the bad (vault). Laying my bag under the bench, I looked back at the beam. A girl even smaller than I was moved quickly through her routine. She was solid until a slight balance check revealed a problem. Just like me, she was on the beam one second and picking herself up off the mat the next.

I found my mom on the bleachers and waved. She sat tall, beautiful, and full of confidence. Her smile told me she already knew what I would do next. I waited until the girl sat down before I made my move.

Glancing around to see if anyone was watching, I walked to where the girl who'd fallen now sat in a chair staring straight ahead. She tried, like I had, to hold in her disappointment so no one could see. I didn't recognize her from any other competitions, but that didn't stop me.

"Hi," I said, a small grin on my face. "I'm Carol."

Looking up at me, her eyes were glassy with unfallen tears. I sat down next to her. "I saw you on beam."

She ducked her head.

"Don't worry about it."

She looked away.

"I fell too." My hands fidgeted on my knees. That got her attention. Her big, round eyes were glued to mine.

"But you got back on and finished," I continued. "Good job." I gave her a smile. "Just . . . show 'em what you've got on the next one. It's vault, right? That's what I'm doing right now." I stood up, brushing my hands on my legs, and smiled, "Good luck."

I heard her quiet "thanks" as I walked back to the vault. I glanced at my family on the bleachers. My mom gave me an approving nod. My dad was already cheering for me, even though I wasn't up yet. My brothers pretended to be indifferent, but I knew they were proud of me.

I don't remember anything else about that meet. I don't know how I did on the vault or what silly jokes my brothers told on the way home. That day, my weakness became my strength. I changed, grew, and learned to get up after a fall. That moment became part of who I was—who I would always be. Moments like that are pit stops, towns, and cities dotting the map of a life's journey that connect long stretches of barren highway. I didn't realize that the events that dotted my map would prepare me for what lay ahead. This one moment of choice—to stand up after a fall—would become a defining characteristic of who I am.

That meet was more than thirty years ago. Since then, my personal journey has taken unexpected turns and tumbles that have brought me to destinations I had never imagined possible. Some moments of impact stand out like beacons of light, while others left me unsure of my ability to keep moving forward. My travels would take me to unbelievable depths of darkness. The journey—my life—has not been defined by the tragedy that struck me and my family but by the joy and beauty we've found in unexpected places. Despite all that has happened, I choose to stand. I choose to be whole—for mine is a life unshattered.

CHAPTER 2

Shattered

Shatter:
To cause to break or burst suddenly into pieces,
as with a violent blow. To damage seriously; disable.
To cause the destruction or ruin of; destroy.
—The Free Dictionary

The soft whisper of air blowing over the hairs on my arm was enough to make me flinch. Muted colors, concrete walls, and glass windows seemed out of place for the panic building inside me. Frightened thoughts churned against one another as I gripped the wheelchair's armrest. The slight movement of my body as I shifted to get more comfortable sent shock waves from my fevered head to my toes. Every bit of me—muscles, joints, skin—everything hurt when I moved.

As the nurse pushed me across the sky bridge from my doctor's office toward the hospital, my husband Scott's gentle touch never left my shoulder. I cupped the underside of my swollen, pregnant belly as another contraction overpowered me. They shouldn't be happening yet. At only thirty-three weeks, it wasn't time.

I'd had a baby before. It hadn't felt like this.

There was something more at work.

Scott leaned close to my ear and whispered, "It's going to be okay, Carol." The deep tones of his voice soothed my frayed nerves.

When the nurse pushed me through the threshold doors of Labor and Delivery, the wheelchair squeaked against the sanitary floors. The whirring of machinery and smell of antiseptic filled my senses. The hospital staff put me in a corner room far from the nurses' station, like a grocery bag they would unpack later.

Confusion and worry overwhelmed me as I watched the nurse strap a monitor around my stomach. The rhythmic beep of the machine monitoring my baby's heartbeat offered some reassurance that the baby was doing all right.

"How long have you had that rash on your face?" The nurse asked as she adjusted the strap on my belly.

"What rash?" I responded through gritted teeth. I looked to Scott, who was peering closely at the side of my face and down my neck.

She took one more look at my face and wrote in her notes but didn't say anything more. A moan escaped my lips as the aching continued to build in my body.

"Can you give her something for pain?" Scott asked.

"Not without permission from the doctor," the nurse said, walking toward the door. "She'll be here in a minute."

Relief couldn't come fast enough, but none was offered. I began to wonder if they knew what was wrong and weren't telling me. Scott looked at me with a raised eyebrow. I could tell he wondered the same thing.

"Scott. . . ." I sucked in a deep breath, trying to weather another contraction. Scott gave me all the comfort he could through my groans and the beeps and hum of the monitor. When the nurse finally came back, I couldn't help myself.

"Can you give me something for the pain, please?" I pleaded, clinging to the side rail. "I ache everywhere."

"The doctor hasn't okayed it yet." She responded with sympathy, but I didn't want it. I wanted relief.

A hint of despair crept into my usually controlled tone. "There has to be something you can give me."

"I'll go ask the doctor again," she said as she left the room.

To fight the emotions churning inside, I tried to ground myself in something, someone. I reached out to grab Scott's hand. I thought I could hold myself together if I held tightly enough. I hoped to keep cracks from forming in the armor of my mental strength. Scott's calm, controlled assurance had been my constant companion for ten years. Surely it could hold me together now.

My hands began to shake as I gripped Scott even tighter. I couldn't understand why the doctor and nurses weren't doing anything to help me. There had to be a pain reliever or drug to stop the contractions. The least they could offer was an answer.

Finally, a different nurse came in, drew blood, and gave me a shot to help relieve my symptoms. While the aching was still there, I could feel a drug-induced calm trickling through my body. For an instant, there was stillness, like a beam of sunshine peeking through the clouds of the storm brewing in my body. Scott gave my hand a squeeze before stepping away to call my mom and let her know the baby was coming.

But the calm didn't last.

The storm couldn't be stopped.

The door burst open. A doctor and five nurses rushed into the room.

"We need to get your baby out now. We're going to prep you," the doctor said without preamble.

"What?" My hold on the side rail tightened as I tried to make sense of what she'd said.

"What's wrong?" Scott asked, rushing back to my bedside.

A nurse started stripping off my clothing. Another pulled out a razor. They moved so fast I couldn't understand what they were doing.

"I need you to sign these papers," another nurse said, handing me paperwork with print so tiny I couldn't read the words.

"Why? What for? Is my baby okay?"

"You have to sign these before we can perform the emergency C-section. Please, we need to go."

The pen was in my hand. I signed. The bed started moving. All I could think about was my baby. Any illusion of control I'd had fled as decisions were no longer mine to make. My only option was to offer a complete surrender of myself. I still didn't know what was causing my symptoms, and no explanations were offered. There simply wasn't time.

They pushed my bed out of the room and down the hall. Fluorescent lights flashed overhead in an eerie striped pattern of light and dark like the scene from a dozen different medical dramas. Only this wasn't television. This was real. I was living a medical emergency that was spinning out of control. The gurney bumped as light and dark continued to lead us down the hall.

I looked at the faces of the people rushing with me—a nurse at each side and Scott behind my head. I could see the fear that flowed through my body reflected in their faces. I turned back, trying to focus on Scott. While he showed little emotion, his eyes—eyes I knew so well—told a different story. Fear broke through his normally cool exterior. When we stopped at the double doors of the operating room, I looked at my husband. The harsh glow of overhead lights couldn't hide the sharp, handsome features of his face.

"Can he come with me?" I asked. I could feel the cracks breaking through my armor, starting small but spreading. I wanted him with me. I needed him by my side.

"No, I'm sorry. He's not allowed." I could hear the regret in her voice.

The cracks deepened, but there wasn't time to argue.

Had I known what was to come, I would have waited, stared, and drunk in every angle, every nuance of the man I married—the curve of his lips, the straightness of his back, the tilt of his head, the look in his eye. I would have burned it all into my memory. But I didn't know. Nobody did.

"You're going to be okay. I'll be here when you get out." Scott said goodbye with a kiss.

A final glance at the doorway was the last time I saw Scott's face with my own eyes.

CHAPTER 3

A Beautiful Life

*"The best and most beautiful things in the world cannot
be seen nor even touched, but just felt in the heart."*
—Helen Keller

He was standing in the doorway of an athletic club the first
time I saw him. His penetrating eyes, slender physique,
and shy smile captured my attention. He wore a tight black
shirt and fashionably well-frayed jeans. My eyes wouldn't leave
him no matter how hard I tried not to stare. Never having
been one to pine or chase after a man, I was caught off guard
by my need to know who he was. I was smitten before I knew
his name.

Through some light investigative work, I discovered Scott's
name, contact information, and class schedule. Back then, the
church-affiliated college we both attended in rural southern
Idaho had all student information available online. My sleuth-
ing made it easy for me to "run into him" on campus. I showed
up outside his classes, crossed his path at the lunch hour, and

strategically placed myself at locations I knew he frequented. I even once chased after him with my backpack open and books spilling out.

I took a chance and casually invited him to stop by the local pizza place where I worked. I know now that Scott wasn't looking for a girlfriend at the time, but he couldn't doubt my interest. Maybe it was curiosity that led him and his brother to my workplace, or maybe his interest was stronger than he let show.

When they walked in, I knew I couldn't waste my chance. I brought breadsticks to their table, a service we didn't usually offer. I acted nonchalant, as if I were surprised to see him there. I threw out my best smile and sparkling conversation. While we said nothing significant, I made some headway.

Back behind the counter, I watched and waited. When they stood up to leave, I hurried from behind the cash register to cut them off.

"Hey, are you guys on your way home?" I asked, steadying my breath after my short sprint.

"Yeah," Scott replied.

His brother tried to hide a smile as he glanced at Scott. I didn't waver in my determination. "So I'm going to a concert in a couple of months." I knew he played percussion in the symphony. "Would you like to go with me?" Hoping he'd know how much I wanted him to accept and also not wanting to wait two months, I continued, "And Sunday I'm making spaghetti. Would you like to come over? Then next week I'm going canoeing with a friend. You wanna go?"

It sounded so much better, more relaxed, less . . .

stalker-like in my head. But the words were out, and I couldn't take them back.

Scott shifted his weight from one foot to the other, his face reddening as he peeked at his brother. For a minute I thought he would run. However, my weeks of innocent pursuit paid off.

"Yeah, okay."

My youthful joy was almost squashed when I realized I'd asked him on three dates at once. "To what?"

"Everything." As he let out a nervous laugh, his smile pulled up higher on the right side in a way that would forever hold my heart.

"Great!" I could hardly play it cool after my eager invitations. Bouncing on my toes, I said, "I'll see you on Sunday, then."

That was the beginning.

Before long, Scott and I became inseparable. The rural farming community that surrounded the college had a charm all its own. A patchwork design of green fields dotted with irrigation sprinklers became the backdrop for many long drives, listening to the grunge music we both loved. It gave us time to have the conversations necessary for a relationship to grow.

As we continued to spend time together, our competitive natures kept our relationship interesting. Our games of Monopoly were epic, eventually getting so heated that to this day we won't play with one another. When we signed up for a cooking class, I had no idea it would turn into another competitive arena for us.

For whatever reason, the cooking professor adored Scott. He could do no wrong in her eyes. When we carved birds out

*Scott and me posing for family
photos at Scott's childhood home.*

of apples, she gushed over his blob that resembled a hockey
puck, giving him an A on the project. Mine, which at least had
wings, got a B. We spent most class periods playfully trying to
outperform one another. Through the class, we discovered a
mutual love of food and passion for cooking. I also gained new
insight into Scott's mischievous nature.

"Make sure you put the knife in the dishwater." I said as I
walked to the front of the classroom carrying both of our plates
to be graded. "Be careful you don't cut yourself." I called over
my shoulder.

"Sure."

I came back to a sink stained red and a knife covered in blood lying haphazardly on the dishwasher rack. Scott sucked air through his teeth as he held his hand dripping with blood over the sink.

"Oh my gosh!" I grabbed a paper towel and tried to stop the bleeding.

As I wiped away blood, his arm quivered in my hands. I thought I was hurting him until I looked at his face and shaking shoulders. He could barely contain his laughter. That's when I noticed the red food coloring lying two feet away on the counter. I punched him in the shoulder, but my loud, distinct laugh could be heard outside of the classroom.

The more I got to know Scott, the more I realized he could be "the one." After six months of dating, I knew my infatuation with him had turned to love. Not one to hold my emotions in, I told him exactly how I felt.

My "I love you" was met with an appreciative nod and an "Oh, thanks." Not the reciprocal declaration I had hoped for.

I tried not to let that bother me. When Scott stroked the back of my hand or touched the small of my back as we walked through a crowd, I knew he cared. For the time being, his feelings were shown through his actions. He once drove two hours to buy a dress I had shown him in a magazine. I was angry with him because for five hours I'd been trying to call him. When he showed up on my doorstep with the brown velvet dress I'd been pining for, it spoke volumes. He also started a tradition of bringing me fresh flowers every week, a tradition that continued long into our married life. His normally stoic voice softened when I entered the room, and his face lit up as our eyes met. This reserved man whom I'd grown to love simply needed more time.

While I waited and hoped Scott would grow to feel the same, I had to break some important news to him. If he was going to be my boyfriend, he had to snowboard. My love of the fresh mountain air and open slopes started at the age of twelve when my older brothers, Heath and Shawn, bought me my first board. I couldn't imagine being in a long-term relationship without sharing my love of the winter breeze whipping past my face as I cut through fresh powder.

Scott took it all in a stride. We signed up for a snowboarding class, figuring we might as well get school credit while doing something fun. However, I ended up providing what little instruction he received. I showed him the basics and let him figure out the rest.

"Get up. Let's go!" I'd say when he face-planted in the snow for the tenth time on a single run. My brothers hadn't been patient teachers, and I saw no reason why I needed to be either.

"Hold on a minute," Scott would say. I'm sure he was catching his breath, but I had a hard time containing my excitement and energy as I waited for him to get up. I wanted to race down the mountain and jump on the chairlift to start all over again.

Luckily, Scott didn't give up, and he was a fast learner. Our drives to the local ski slope provided more time for important conversations that deepened our understanding of one another. Having survived the snowboarding test, our relationship continued to progress until Scott finally spoke the words I'd been waiting for.

It took Scott a full year after my declaration of love to utter an "I love you." They were not flippant words—words he said simply because I had said them first. From Scott, the words "I love you" were analyzed, thought out, and planned before they left his mouth. I let the words wash over me and soak into my soul.

He was mine, and I was his.

Another year and a half later, when Scott and I were looking for separate apartments in a new college town, we ran into some trouble. Neither of us could find roommates. As we looked for a solution, the answer became obvious—move in together. It seemed simple enough.

We spent a long, sweaty day trudging up three flights of stairs with all our earthly possessions. As I panted up and down those stairs, a nagging feeling began to grow that I could not ignore. I was raised in a religious home. Though I hadn't been a practicing member of any faith for quite some time, the values I had learned as a child were deeply embedded in my feelings toward living with someone before marriage. When we finally finished moving the last of our belongings, Scott sat on the couch as I stood in the middle of the room looking at the fruits of our labor.

I turned to him and said, "I can't do this."

"What do you mean?" Scott asked with his head laid back on the couch, taking a much needed breather.

"I don't want to live with you."

That got his attention. He lifted his head and looked at me in surprise.

"I don't want to be your live-in girlfriend. I want to be your wife." I hadn't realized how important marriage was to me until I stopped and looked at what we were about to do.

"Are you serious?" he asked.

Though I could hear the disbelief in his voice, I couldn't ignore a gnawing deep inside that this was an important moment for us as a couple. It was time for a step forward, not sideways.

"Yes," I said without hesitation.

He didn't speak, and his face remained shocked, maybe a little annoyed. Finally he spoke. "Really? You couldn't have told me that before we moved everything to the third floor?"

I went home to eastern Washington while Scott returned to his home in western Washington. We began the task of planning a wedding in only two and a half months. Ultimately, we both wanted to get married, and though our decision to do so had come in an unconventional way, Scott was determined to follow tradition. He wouldn't formally ask me to marry him until he asked my dad, in person, for my hand in marriage.

Six weeks after we'd left school, in front of Scott's family home with his mother and sister watching from the window, Scott proposed. I was supposed to travel the four hours back home but had to stay an extra hour for some time with him. I was lucky not to get in a car accident when I drove home, as I couldn't take my eyes off of my engagement ring.

A short time later, we were married. But marriage didn't mark the end of change or growth for us.

I trained as a medical assistant while Scott completed his bachelor's degree in molecular cell biology. He was soon accepted to a dental school in Boston. Moving across the country proved to be one of the most difficult experiences of my life to that point. I've never handled change well, and moving was full of unknowns. We found an apartment a week before we

Shawn, me, Scott, and Heath on our wedding day, March 14, 1998.

arrived, but neither of us had a job when we got there. We didn't have family in the area to fall back on, only each other.

I had never experienced what it was like to know nobody. I waved at the neighbors as we moved into a large apartment complex. No one waved back or even said hello. Scott and I grew up in rural communities where a friendly hello was expected, but Boston was a different experience. I spent the first week trying to navigate the subway system as I traveled from one job interview to the next.

I found a job working fifty hours a week at the Massachusetts General Hospital Diabetes Center. My work there brought me into contact with people from all over the world, including some brilliant doctors and nurses. There was one doctor, a prestigious endocrinologist, who made a point of regularly asking me how I was doing. He showed concern when I had a rough day and treated everyone with the same consideration and kindness. His encouragement kept me hopeful when I felt isolated and alone in a strange city.

Though I was grateful for the job, I barely made enough to cover our expenses.

"What are we going to do?" I asked Scott as he looked at his school schedule. Scott's class load didn't leave time for a part-time job. "Should I look for a second job?"

Scott's brow furrowed. "That's one option, but we'd hardly see each other." He thought for a second longer. "We could sell my car. We can both take the subway to work and school."

That got the ideas rolling. We used what little savings we had to pay off my car and reduce our debt and monthly expenses as much as possible so we could live off my salary.

We rode the subway early each day, separating with a kiss. I looked for Scott's familiar figure waiting for me at the station when the train pulled in at six or seven each evening. Our time together was so limited that daily chores became our bonding time. We shopped for groceries, did household cleaning, and listened to one another's frustrations after our tiring days.

What little extra money we had was strategically saved for special occasions. Our favorite treat was to try a new restaurant. We sampled everything from the cheapest diner to expensive seven-course meals at the renowned Radius. For us, eating out was about more than the food. It was about the experience—the smell of tiger lilies in the lobby, the music, lights, arrangement of the food on the plate, and creative flavor combinations.

During our first year in Boston, a feeling grew in me. Maybe it was the biological ticking of my clock, or it could have been my loneliness while I waited for Scott to finish studying each day, but I couldn't deny a growing desire to start a family. I wanted a greater purpose in my life—motherhood. I was close to my mother and wanted to have the same strong influence in the life of my children that she had in mine. I daydreamed about not only teaching our children to snowboard and cook but also telling them how those activities had brought their parents together.

I loved children. In fact, I'd strongly considered becoming a teacher but gave up that ambition when I realized my tender heart would break watching some children return to destructive or dangerous homes at the end of the school day. I wouldn't be able to save them all, which is why I turned to a medical profession in which my compassion was needed but my heart stayed safe.

The pull to nurture was so strong that a year after we moved to Boston, I told Scott, "We either need to have a baby or get a cat because I can't take this much longer."

We got a beautiful tabby named Ralph who kept me company while Scott studied.

We also moved to an apartment closer to the city, where we found ourselves part of a thriving young professional community. Boston wasn't the friendliest city, but once we became a part of it, we made lifelong friendships. I love where I live now, but Boston will always hold a special place in my heart.

Three years later, when Scott was done with school and we'd moved back to Washington, where I worked at a cardiac center in Seattle, the time was right for a family. We'd been married for eight years by that time.

Scott was away at a dental conference. My mom and

I were out on one of our all-day shopping trips. We usually started at ten in the morning and collapsed through the front door twelve hours later. I started strong, but as the day went on, I grew fatigued to the point that I wasn't sure I could keep going.

Mid-afternoon I told my mom, "I have to go home. I'm so tired."

She looked surprised. I'd never backed out on a shopping trip. "Are you feeling okay?"

"I'm sure I'm fine." I had my suspicions, but I wanted to wait until I talked to Scott and knew for sure.

I could hardly wait for him to come home so we could confirm my pregnancy together.

Trying to rein in my excitement, I bounded out of the bathroom and exclaimed, "We're pregnant!"

His, "Wow. Okay, yeah," was followed with a simple, "We're going to have a baby." He thought a bit longer, his smile growing. "Yeah, that's great." There was a tenderness in his eyes I'd never seen before, and his hug was longer than usual, as though he couldn't bear to let me go.

The next weekend we went to a bookstore, where Scott headed straight for the baby books. He found the usual first pregnancy books, baby naming books, and even a book that was just about a woman who was pregnant. That evening, and many evenings after, we sat on our patio reading baby books together.

To say that I had the glow of pregnancy would be an understatement. It was more like the glaring lights of joy and happiness shone blindingly bright wherever I went.

"Carol," my coworker would laughingly reprimand, "you

are strutting. I don't think you're supposed to wear high heels when you're pregnant."

"Well, I'm going to," I said, admiring my chunky Mary Janes. "I love them." I felt great, loved my pregnant body, and walked in my high heels through to full term. An uncomplicated pregnancy led to an uncomplicated birth.

From the second I saw my Chloe Jean, I was in love. I stared at her dark hair and long eyelashes as we dimmed the lights in the hospital room. The fireworks of Seattle's New Year's Eve celebration lit up our room, creating a sense of euphoric happiness I'd never experienced. The beginning of a new year marked the start of a new chapter in our lives.

Chloe's life was a gift, and I stared at her for hours. As her perfect little body slept in my arms, I stroked her cheek and marveled that she was mine. I found peace and joy as I spent all day, every day with her. Working in the medical field fulfilled my need to help others, but raising my daughter brought the purpose I'd longed for. Chloe and Scott made me whole. We created an unbreakable bond that only grew stronger with time. My days reading books, singing, laughing, and playing with Chloe brought a contentedness to my life I hadn't known was missing. I was living the life I'd dreamed about for years.

Eleven months later we got an unexpected but not unwanted surprise. I was pregnant again. Scott was excited in his reserved way, while I was a little embarrassed. I had often, and loudly, declared I would never get pregnant right after having a baby. I didn't stay embarrassed for long. I knew another baby could only add more joy. As we prepared to welcome a new baby, we moved out of a rental house into an affordable home of our own.

Cuddling with Chloe shortly after she was born.

My second pregnancy wasn't as easy physically as the first, but nothing could dampen our excitement as we prepared. I wanted this new little girl to feel as special and loved as Chloe. We sold my car to pay for new baby furniture. I washed, folded, and put all her clothes in the dresser drawers long before her due date. When I wasn't preparing for the baby, I was taking care of Chloe, settling into our new home, and running our household. Like any expectant mother, I imagined what the new baby would look like and how her arrival would change our family.

With a new home, loving husband, adorable daughter, and baby on the way, it was truly a beautiful life.

CHAPTER 4

A Broken Vessel

*"A fine glass vase goes from treasure to trash, the moment
it is broken. Fortunately, something else happens to you and
me. Pick up your pieces. Then, help me gather mine."*
—Vera Nazarian

No amount of shaking my head could clear a path through
the heavy fog of sedation. In a way, the medically-
induced coma protected me from the mental and physical anguish of feeling my body destroy itself from the inside out. But
on the flip side, I didn't witness the shattering of my life. I was
left in confusion with unanswered questions.

My memory of the first twenty days after the emergency
C-section is almost nonexistent save for a few fragmented
moments. Most of what I now know comes from family and
friends who were there, watching firsthand as our lives were
changed forever.

The C-section itself took only ten minutes. Afterward, a
nurse ushered Scott into the operating room to catch a brief
glimpse of our baby before she was whisked away to the

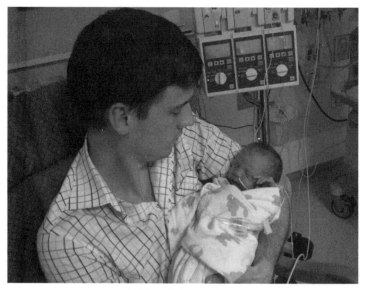

Scott holding Safiya in the hospital.

Neonatal Intensive Care Unit (NICU). Once there, a feeding tube was inserted, and they fought to keep the baby's blood pressure up. At four pounds, fifteen ounces, she was large for a preemie but tiny in comparison to a full-term baby. Her future, like mine, was uncertain.

Scott waited, watching other families of surgery patients come and go as news of their loved ones came. Nervous energy escaped through a rhythmic tapping of his foot, leftover from his years as a drummer. He tried to read magazines or watch the television, but he couldn't focus. He kept family updated and made a trip to the NICU to see the baby again. As he watched the clock on his phone, he didn't know the long wait was unusual for a C-section. The only news he'd received of my condition came from a nurse who had told him that there were complications and they were trying to stabilize my blood pressure.

Three hours later, I was moved to the Intensive Care Unit (ICU), where nurses struggled to get a central line into my neck to monitor my blood pressure and quickly administer antibiotics. An exhausted Scott was brought to my room with a growing dread that something was drastically wrong. Dr. Solomon, the ICU doctor, took the time to pull him aside to be sure he understood the severity of the situation.

"Mr. Decker, your wife has sepsis. More specifically, she's in septic shock, which has caused her blood pressure to plummet."

"Is it serious?"

With a heavy sigh and a practiced bedside manner, Dr. Solomon tried to remain professional as he gave news he knew no spouse wanted to hear. "Yes. Sepsis releases toxins into the blood. Those toxins are spreading to every part of your wife's body. Her body is basically attacking itself. If we can't get her blood pressure stable and find the source of her infection, I don't know if she'll make it."

The blood drained from Scott's face. "What are you doing to stabilize her blood pressure?"

"We're using drugs called vasopressors to bring her blood pressure up. We've had to use more than one because she's not responding right away. We've also given her extra fluids." He hesitated before continuing, "Vasopressors have dangerous side effects, especially the longer she takes them. I wouldn't give them to her if I thought there was another option. You may notice some discoloration of her extremities—nose, ears, fingertips, and toes. She's going to start to swell with all the extra fluid. You might want to prepare yourself and anyone who comes to visit regarding what to expect when they see her. The sooner we get her stable, the better."

At 3:00 a.m., after an MRI, more tests, and medication, my blood pressure held steady as the vasopressors started to work. Finally, the room quieted, providing the first solitary moments for Scott to think. As tired as he was, sleep wouldn't come. He tried to make sense of what was happening as he absorbed the fact that half of sepsis patients don't survive.

The word *sepsis* originates from a Greek word meaning "decay" or "putrefy." It is an aggressive response by the immune system to an infection. The toxins it causes lead to inflammation in all the major organs, effectively bringing on decay from the inside out. Two days after my C-section, doctors discovered my initial flu-like symptoms had been caused by streptococcal pneumoniae, which triggered sepsis.

Within the first few days, I was put on dialysis because my kidneys had stopped working. My heart was affected, pumping out a fraction of the blood needed to sustain my extremities. I also developed disseminated intravascular coagulation (DIC). Essentially, my body was shutting down in an attempt to save my vital organs.

DIC alone is so deadly that amongst ICU nurses it carries the nickname of "Death Is Coming." It caused blood clots to spread throughout my body, lodging in both of my calves as well as my left wrist and right ring finger. Lack of blood flow spread the discoloration of my skin from the vasopressors even further. Because of the clotting from DIC, when I did need to clot, the necessary proteins were depleted. I started bleeding through my C-section incision as well as my mouth. When

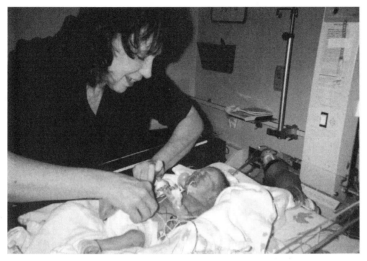

My mom, Darla, with Safiya.

nothing seemed to help, an experimental drug that required the approval of six different doctors was ordered. It didn't work either.

Smaller clots sporadically appeared under my skin, causing dark patches of dead, sloughing skin on my arms, legs, and abdomen. In total, a third of my body would eventually need skin grafts to repair the damage.

Additionally, my fever soared to 106.9 degrees. With the high fever and blood clots visibly affecting my body, the doctors worried about brain damage. The medically-induced coma prevented them from knowing for sure.

The only indication I gave of normal brain function was the grimace that crossed my face each time I was moved. After an MRI showed no visible clots in my brain, they reduced my sedation to see if I showed signs of responding. As the medication left my system, I groaned and tossed in bed. Occasionally

I became agitated despite Scott and the medical staff trying to calm me.

After five days, the vasopressors were stopped. The color and warmth of my extremities was closely monitored, especially my feet and left hand. On a good day, my feet looked lighter in color and the pulse could be found. But my condition was far from stable. The heavy medication I needed depressed my brain functions so that it didn't tell my body to breathe. An intubation tube that reached from my airway to a ventilator kept my lungs filled with oxygen. My temperature would skyrocket and my blood pressure would drop with no discernible cause or explanation. Life would start to pull away from me without warning.

Scott sat by my bedside, fighting to keep hope in view.

"Guess what they said today?" he'd say, tucking my hair behind my ear away from the tube in my mouth. My face so swollen he could hardly recognize me, he'd continue, "They said you *might* make it. It doesn't sound like much, but it's better than, 'We don't know if she'll make it.' You can do this. I love you."

Other days he talked about the normal aspects of the life we'd shared before sepsis.

"I decided on a name today. Safiya. It's Swahili for 'pure or sincere friend.' Do you remember that one from our list? Safiya Christian, so she'll have my initials just like Chloe has yours. She's beautiful and a fighter. She pushed her bottle away and hit one of the nurses today. I can't wait for you to meet her."

Brief, less medicated moments came during breathing trials, in which they tested my ability to breathe on my own. The intubation tube was removed and medication decreased. Daily breathing trials offered short periods of consciousness that I mostly don't remember. They proved to be difficult for me and my family. Reduced sedation left me crying as I asked for Scott and the girls or to go home. One time the medication left my system so fast I became agitated and tried to get up.

Not for the first time, Scott explained to me, "Carol, you're in the hospital."

"Why? I want to go home." Weak movements and slow blinks were all I could manage.

"You're sick, remember? You have to stay here."

"No. I want to go home. I want to leave." I lifted my foot three feet in the air, letting it crash down onto the bed with surprising force.

"Let me out! Take me home! I want to go home!"

Scott and the nurse held me in bed until the medication took over again. The intubation tube would then be snaked back down my throat.

Each time I woke, I came closer to remembering why I was there and what had happened. One of those brief moments of clarity stuck with me. I can't forget the first time I met my baby girl.

"Carol, how are you feeling?" Scott's soft whisper was so close I could almost feel his breath on my skin.

I tried to respond but couldn't speak. Images pushed their way to the forefront of my memory. A kiss from Scott. Doors closing. Machines. Lights. People rushing. The baby . . . my baby.

Where was she?

As I moved to look for her, the crinkling of heavy plastic from the special therapeutic bed distracted my focus and added to my muddled thinking. The bed was meant to prevent bed sores, but I didn't know that at the time. It was just one more sensation I didn't understand. A motor startled me as it burst to life blowing up a balloon underneath my leg—yet another out-of-place noise.

I knew I should be in the hospital. It smelled like a hospital, but the sounds and how I felt were wrong. The confusion created a barrier between me and my baby.

Scott moved closer. "Try to stay quiet. Are you hurting?"

I shook my head no. My discomfort seemed irrelevant to finding my baby. I needed words, but I couldn't make them.

I needed to ask how she was, to know she was okay. I searched the shadows of dark, patches of light, and shapes I didn't recognize. The urge to get out of bed and tear apart the room was powerful. Weak muscles and unresponsive limbs only added to the list of obstacles keeping me in place. I strained to see through the haze, hoping Scott would recognize the yearning in my eyes.

"Hey." His voice was so close he must have been only inches from my face. The perfect image I had of him in my mind made every feature look handsome, confident, and strong. "Are you worried about the baby?"

I put on the most enthusiastic face I could muster and nodded my head. I loved him even more for knowing me so well.

"She's beautiful, and she's doing fine."

Relief flooded from my heart through to the rest of me, but that didn't stop me from trying to raise my head, hoping to see her. The only thing in the room I could make out with any detail was Scott, but even then it was like I was looking at him through wax paper. No matter how hard I squinted or blinked, I couldn't wash away the film on my eyes.

"She's not in here right now." His voice was gentle and slow, as though he chose his words carefully.

That can't be right, I thought. *They always keep the baby in the mother's room.*

I grew agitated and restless as I continued to try to see her. Scott's hands rested on my shoulders, holding me in place. I couldn't understand why he would keep me from my baby.

"Please, Carol," he said, the calm dissipating from his tone. "You're sick. You can't get out of bed. She's not here in the room."

I could hear shuffling and whispers. "We can get her," said an urgent feminine voice I didn't recognize. "It won't take long."

The last wisps of fog clung to the corners of my thinking. With so many strange sounds and smells, I had barely noticed there were other people in the room.

"I'll go get her," Scott replied with his head turned away from me.

More than one pair of shoes squeaked as a curtain was thrown back, followed by the opening of a heavy door. As they left, it closed as though sealing a portal through which I couldn't pass.

The anticipation of waiting was almost more than I could bear. I needed to know for myself that the baby was okay. *She's coming*, I told myself over and over. I wondered if she had dark hair and eyes like Chloe or if she had my nose and Scott's chin.

I wanted to tell Scott I felt strange—my legs heavy, my hands like clubs, my eyes blurred. But he was getting our baby, I reminded myself.

I tried to sit up, but nothing happened.

Waiting, immobile, in the strange bed, my searching eyes and sluggish brain tried to make sense of it all. Opening and closing my eyelids did nothing to bring the room into focus.

Trying to sit up again, I managed a weak flop that turned my head to the other side. When I tried to push up with my arms, they didn't work. I didn't know my hands and feet lay black and lifeless.

Outside my room, a flurry of nurses ignored protocol to prepare Safiya for the trip to my room. Bringing her may have seemed simple to me, but it took the concentrated efforts of nurses in the ICU and NICU. Taking a preemie from the NICU to the ICU is rarely, if ever, done. The thread of life I clung to was so thin, many of the nurses feared this would be our only meeting as mother and daughter on this earth.

When the door opened, I widened my eyes, attempting to see her.

"Here she is," said Scott with clear affection in his voice. From across the room he talked softly to a tiny bundle.

A quiet peace overcame me as time lost meaning.

I had waited months to meet this little girl. The final few feet seemed like miles. It was enough to make me want to jump up, pull her to my chest, and hum my love to her. I didn't want to scare her, but the effort it took to quiet myself nearly made my heart burst. I wanted to reach for her. Hold her. But my clubby hands and arms stayed frustratingly at my sides. Useless.

Tiny grunts and squeaks drifted ahead of her. Her sweet baby sounds moved over my raw nerves like a balm. Small and quiet but unrestrained, her coos filled the void between us. Finally, I breathed the scent of untouched purity that only accompanies a newborn. It lazily drifted over me, forging that intangible but unbreakable connection between mother and child.

"Meet Safiya," Scott said, his voice thick with emotion.

Tears fell as he brought us together. Cheek to cheek. Mother to daughter. Soul to soul.

The image of a dark-haired baby filled my mind. Whether it was really her or only my brain's creation, I don't know. And it doesn't matter. It was enough.

Long eyelashes brushed against my face, opening and closing in a sleepy, rhythmic pattern. The soft, supple skin of her ear pressed against my cheek, forming to my shape. A thin, wrinkled hand brushed my nose as tiny fingers curled into a fist. Her delicate baby hair tickled my ear as I shifted my head to nuzzle her, but I couldn't give the kiss I longed to give. Love, gratitude, and hope collided as we spent our first minutes together as a family.

I wanted to stay there with Safiya and Scott, away from the strange sounds, sterile smells, and chaos of the hospital. After I'd felt her skin against mine, adrenaline began to subside, leaving exhaustion in its place. Heavy with a tiredness fueled by medication, I started to drift off before the baby was taken from the room. I tried to make the words to say I loved her. But no sound escaped the intubation tube. As quickly as Safiya had come, she was gone through the heavy door with a blurry stranger.

Our meeting was brief but left me with a sense of completion. Yet my body wasn't whole, and my mind drifted in and out of reality.

Over the next two weeks, the doctors and Scott began to notice something unusual. As doctors explained my progress or Scott told me about Safiya, I looked past them without making eye contact. An ICU doctor began regularly checking the dilation of my eyes. At first they dilated normally, but within a few days, they had stopped. My pupils remained large, as though trying to let in more light.

The doctor finally asked, "Can you see my hand?"

I immediately answered, "Yes." It was a strange phenomenon. My brain didn't know I couldn't see and would project images of what it knew it should see. I wasn't lucid enough with the heavy medication to know I wasn't seeing reality.

"Okay. Can you follow the light with your eyes, please?"

Nothing. The right questions made it obvious that my eyes weren't properly working. A specialist was called for further examination.

"The eyes are healthy," he told us on first examination. "But the optic nerve is damaged. Normally it is pink, but it has started to turn yellow. If you picture the eyes like a video camera, the electrical cord is there but isn't working."

"Can anything be done?" Scott asked while I listened silently.

"Right now, no. It may be a temporary side effect of the vasopressors or the sepsis, although this isn't a usual complication. It could take as long as twelve to eighteen months to know for sure."

Medically, there was so much happening that the idea of permanent blindness was more than I could absorb at the time. Because I knew my sight *could* come back, I didn't focus on my blindness. My other physical problems, which caused

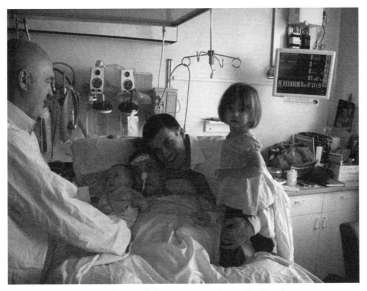

At the hospital during a visit from the family.

more pain, took all my attention. Scott didn't push the subject. Blindness wasn't something I would be ready to accept and deal with for months. It wasn't something I think he was ready to accept either.

Looking back at the broken pieces of my life, I realize that mine was not the only life that shattered.

Scott stayed with me as much as he could, but he also had Safiya in the hospital and eighteen-month-old Chloe at home, who missed her mom and dad. His parents took care of Chloe during the day, and Scott tried to eat dinner with her before he came to see me at night. He'd also bought his own dental practice the year before, which meant he had a responsibility to care for his employees. His life became a precarious balancing act. Heavy decisions weighed on his shoulders. He faced them with unbelievable strength and courage.

The effects of sepsis and its complications left Scott with some difficult choices to make. Talk of amputation began to enter the conversation when the dark coloring on my feet began to spread up my legs. The viability of my left hand was also still in question. Scott brought in different doctors for second, third, and fourth opinions, hoping someone would know how to save all of me.

Scott struggled as the thought of making a life-altering decision for his wife cut into his conscience. He didn't want to make that choice without getting my input, even though I was in no condition to give any.

"Carol?" Scott whispered as I came out of sedation once again.

With eyes glazed over, I looked in his direction with hints of fear and confusion.

"Do you remember how I told you about sepsis? The blood clots?"

Slow, heavy blinks met his determined gaze. His voice caught as he forced his emotions under control.

"You're running a fever, and your blood pressure is dropping again. The doctors think it's because of your feet, where they're turning black. Your body is fighting it like an infection."

Rolling my head the other direction and lifting a limp arm wasn't much of a response.

"Hey," Scott called my attention back to his face. "The doctors want to amputate your feet, both of them, to save your life. I just . . . I don't want to make that decision until I've talked to you. If we wait too much longer, you might not make it. . . . I think it's the right thing to do." A gentle stroke of my hair and cheek brought my eyes to where I thought his face was.

"I'm sorry," he said. "I wish there were another way. I keep looking but . . . I'm sorry. I love you."

Scott wasn't really expecting an answer, and I don't remember the conversation. He was riddled with doubt and questions. Would I survive? Would I blame him for the loss of my feet? Was there another alternative he and the doctors hadn't considered?

In the meantime, my condition continued to worsen. With a racing heart, constant fever, and fluctuating blood pressure, the outcome wasn't looking good. The blackness on my feet continued to spread, creeping ever closer to my knees. Removing my feet would take away the source of the infection, allowing my body to start the healing process and stabilizing my vital signs. Scott waited to make the final decision until it couldn't be avoided. Despite some differing opinions amongst the family, a week after the doctors had initially scheduled the amputations, Scott finally consented.

By the time he had made the choice, it was not a quality of life issue anymore. He wanted me to live, and amputation was his last hope.

He chose life.

My feet were amputated—the left just above my ankle and the right mid-calf. It was only three weeks after I'd had Safiya. It was a dark day for Scott and my family. Once my feet were removed, my temperature dropped, my heartbeat slowed, and my blood pressure stabilized for a time. As hard as it had been, amputation was the right choice.

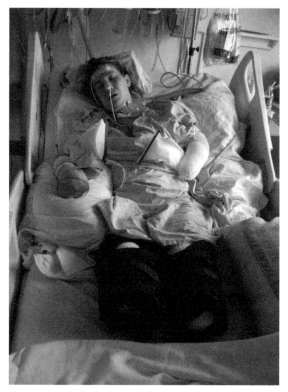

Lying in the hospital bed after my amputations.

It wasn't the last time Scott would be faced with the decision to amputate. My left hand and right ring finger were still dark, but with medication that improved circulation, there was hope they could still be saved.

However, waiting on my hand to recover pushed back the treatment needed for the dark patches of skin that still covered my body. These needed debridement—removal of the dead skin from the wounds caused by DIC—and skin grafts, much like a severe burn would. The doctors didn't consider my condition stable enough to begin this process until they knew whether I would lose my hand. It was a frustrating waiting game—one in which only time would tell the outcome.

I hadn't known when I entered the hospital with early labor contractions that my beautiful life was about to shatter. But now, pieces were about to start drifting back to me, starting with consciousness. Others, literal pieces, like my feet, would never return. Still others I would have to work, sweat, and bleed to find again.

When I met Safiya, it marked the beginning of periodic awakenings that grew more frequent and longer in duration. Groggy and disoriented, my body full of more hurt, confusion, and loss than I had imagined was possible for one person to bear, I tried to make sense of my condition. My family held my life together for me because I couldn't do it on my own. My fight for survival was only beginning as I was faced with the question: What do you do with the shattered pieces of a once beautiful life?

CHAPTER 5

Foundations of Love

"Love has no boundary, no limitation of good will."
—*David B. Haight*

Pieces of my former life—Chloe, my home, and my family—carried over into a new scattered existence with little order, only uncertainty. There was nothing left to do but flow through the days—in and out of consciousness, in and out of my life. The doctors had saved me from drowning in the effects and complications of sepsis, but neither Scott nor I could hold our lives together on our own. Physically broken and mentally fragile, I needed support far beyond my own means. Scott couldn't possibly be everywhere and provide for everyone that needed him, either.

Family, friends, and devoted medical staff created a foundation of support. They held the shards of my life together while I struggled to survive.

Within a week of my illness, my brother Heath quit his

job in Texas. He moved back to Washington to be with me at the hospital while Scott worked. Though six foot four, with an imposing presence, Heath brushed my hair, wiped tears, and held my hand before procedures. He massaged my hands to stimulate the circulation and lifted my spirits. His confidence in me and my recovery made me believe I could do anything. I focused on his voice, the feel of his skin, or the smell of his cologne to control my panic. Having him there when Scott couldn't be offered much needed peace of mind.

After the amputation of my feet, my condition stabilized enough to start debridement. Fifteen patches on my arms, legs, and abdomen—approximately thirty percent of my body—needed skin grafts. The wounds looked and acted like severe burns and had to be treated as such. Thankfully, I was sedated, but going to and waking up from procedures left me dazed and confused.

Shaking my head, I'd beg Heath with my eyes not to let them take me again. I may not remember what they did, but when I woke I could feel the burning sensation ready to overcome the medication's ability to hide my discomfort. A wrong touch or movement could send sharp, piercing waves through my body. Once the pain started, it could take hours to get under control.

Heath was strong for me when I couldn't be. Small changes in my daily routine caused me to break into tears. All the changes in my life made it difficult to cope with any unknown.

"I'll be here when you wake up," Heath would say with his deep, tranquil voice. "Don't worry." Those were the words he used the day I had my intubation tube replaced by a tracheotomy tube. The procedure should have been a relief. Day after

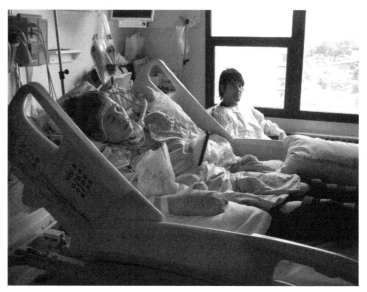

Heath at my bedside, where he stayed every day.

day I listened as people around me carried on conversations with each other and talked *at* me.

"Carol, would you like another blanket?" my mother would ask.

I would shake my head no. I couldn't regulate my body temperature, leaving me perpetually overheated.

"Are you hurting? Do you need more pain medication?" Scott was always so concerned with my pain level. I would shake my head no.

All I could do was respond to their yes-or-no questions, when I wanted to ask if it was sunny outside and who was watching Chloe. I wondered how Safiya was doing, but I had no way to ask. Isolated and alone, I missed and needed words to become part of the world again.

A trach tube fits into the throat through an incision in the front of the neck. It would allow me to breathe without the use of my nose or mouth during procedures and meant I wouldn't need to be intubated for all the upcoming surgeries. When not in use, the tube would remain in place but could be closed, which would allow me to talk. I wanted words back, but the unknown brought more anxiety. I was afraid I'd wake up to find my condition even worse.

Heath held me together, shared his courage, and offered me strength when I had none.

"It's going to be okay," he whispered, sensing my growing apprehension. "You can do this. I know you can." Confidence, hope, and faith moved through his voice, seeping their way into me.

I'd grown used to the cloudiness of waking from anesthesia, but when I woke with the trach tube, I was surprised by the pressure on my chest. I wasn't used to breathing on my own, and I found I had to force air into my lungs. Fighting the feeling of suffocation, I needed to relax and trust that my lungs would work again, but panic began to build.

Heath drew close and whispered, "Shhh. It's going to be okay. Slow down. Try to relax. Slow breaths."

Nurses talked in the background, but all I could hear was Heath.

"Remember what we talked about? Deep, slow breaths."

"Heath," I said—*I said! My voice.* I'd spoken without thinking. Disuse had left my vocal chords weak. The tube sticking out of my neck made me want to clear my throat. But after only four hours I was able to put together short sentences.

Unshattered

"I don't know if I can . . ." I paused to breathe. " . . . do it, Heath."

"Just breathe. Breathe." He exaggerated his breathing, demonstrating the pattern we'd discussed before the surgery. As I tried to draw air in, I listened to his voice and the rhythmic rise and fall of his chest. I knew he wouldn't let me fail. My struggle to breathe made me remember a trip we'd made to Hawaii for my brother Shawn's wedding. Heath and I had gone out on the reef of Hanauma Bay to snorkel. An inexperienced snorkeler, I had panicked and hyperventilated, brushing Heath's leg as I started to flail. He turned, looked at me with reassurance in his eyes, and motioned for me to follow. Trying to breathe through the trach tube, I imagined his eyes boring into me with the same confidence he'd shown on the reef. It wasn't long before our chests rose and fell in unison.

If Heath knew I could do it, I could. And I did.

"Heath." My throat was scratchy and dry. It didn't feel natural like it had before. Then again, nothing felt like before.

Heath's voice thickened with emotion when he said, "There you are. It's good to hear your voice."

"I . . ." I sucked in a gulp of air. " . . . sound weird."

"That'll get better, and you sound amazing. Keep breathing, in and out."

I followed his breathing. I practiced taking deep breaths and then speaking, as I couldn't do both at the same time.

Calm and focused, words were now mine to use.

"Great," Heath said, rubbing his hands together, "now we'll have a surprise for Scott."

"What?"

"He thought it might take you a few days to talk with the

trach tube, but the nurses and I knew you could do it sooner. We're going to call him, and you're going to talk to him on the phone."

My stomach fluttered. Surprising Scott with good news after so much bad seemed like a gift from heaven. Heath reached into the pocket of his jeans to get his phone. As he held it to my ear, a rush of adrenaline washed over my system.

"Hello?" Scott's strong, clear voice said in my ear.

"Hi, honey," I rasped.

Silence.

I wondered if the cell phone had dropped the call. "Scott?" I asked.

"Carol?"

"Yeah."

His happy laugh rang out in my ear.

"They got it out okay?" I could hear the smile in his voice.

"Yes."

"It's good to hear your voice." He paused. "I can't believe I'm talking to you."

"Yeah, me neither." I took big breaths, preparing for a multiple-word answer.

An excitement I hadn't heard in his tone for far too long filled his words. "I'll be up there as soon as I get off work."

"No, don't do that." As much as I wanted to see him, I didn't want to be more of a burden.

Scott laughed, "Why not?"

"You've been at work." I took a breath, saying words I didn't feel. "You have . . . Chloe to worry about. I'm okay. You don't . . . need to come." Every sentence was broken by my labored efforts.

With his voice full of laughter, he said, "Right. I love you. Bye."

"Bye," I whispered.

Ignoring my excuses for him to stay away, Scott walked through the door of my room two hours later. A girlish giddiness, like I'd felt the first time I had met him, filled me as I used my newly found voice to speak.

Scott made the hour-long drive from our home in Enumclaw to Seattle almost every day. Even though the long drives to the hospital were exhausting, they provided an important escape for him. He didn't have to be strong or quiet or patient in the car. The powerful mix of emotions he experienced was released in the relative safety of a moving vehicle. All the demands and decisions that filled every part of his life were put on hold while he drove.

After feeding and rocking Safiya, he would spend the rest of the evening with me. Sometimes he stayed the night in my room; other evenings he went back home to be with Chloe. While I drifted in and out of consciousness, he updated a blog he'd started a week after I was admitted to the hospital. He used it to keep family and friends informed of my status. It helped cut down the time he spent on the phone and proved to be a therapeutic way for him to sort through the events of each day. His blog followers expanded to include nurses from the hospital, community members, and strangers. Words of encouragement and support flooded in.

These people offered true charity. The word *charity* usually creates images of people giving money, which in my case also happened. But true charity is more than monetary support. For us, it came in the form of acceptance and love unhindered by superficial differences. Others saw what we had in common rather than what made us different. When strangers heard my story, they saw me as a daughter, sister, and mother who couldn't see her baby, struggling through daily suffering. Because many of them had experienced suffering themselves, they empathized and wanted to help relieve my troubles.

Charity and support didn't have to come in large, grand gestures, although sometimes it did come that way, like when Heath left his job. People offered charity by taking the time to let Scott and me know they cared. Prayers, meals, and words of kindness bolstered our spirits and helped us feel connected to others even when our daily routine kept us isolated.

Scott would often lie next to me in bed reading comments left on the blog by well-wishers. Some were friends from the past:

"Scott, you don't know me but . . . I went to school with Carol . . . and heard the horrible news. [I] wanted to let you know that I will be praying for your family. Carol is a fighter and [I'm] glad to hear she is doing better. I will keep Carol in my prayers."

Others were strangers leaving their support:

"I am reading your entire blog right now and am just stunned. Scared, awed, everything. It's times like this that I wish I were religious—then I would know how to pray for you and your family. But I'm not, I don't. I hope it's enough that I am sending you all healthy healing courageous energy."

People rallied behind us in ways we never could have imagined:

"I have been emailing friends all over the country asking

for their good thoughts and prayers. There are so many people with you in their thoughts, as we are!"

Knowing that so many people cheered and hoped for our family built a bridge between us and the outside world. I didn't know how much the support of others could lift in times of tragedy until I was the one who needed it. The inherent goodness of people and their willingness to share their love made a difference. My whole family experienced the power of charity.

The hope and positivity of others strengthened us, giving us courage when the tide of adversity washed over us again. My left hand and right ring finger continued to deteriorate. Scott brought several experts to see me in the hope that my hand and finger could be saved. In the end, amputation was the only option.

The day before the surgery, several of my high school girl-friends came to visit. The nurses told them I was too heavily sedated to hear them. But my memory of their visit is so clear I was sure I interacted with them. They entered the hospital with contagious energy. I drank it in even as I floated in and out of consciousness.

"Do you remember all of us piling into your old brown truck, Carol?" Nicole asked. "What was it? Four in the front and two in the back?"

Kim added, "I'm surprised the doors didn't burst open, there were so many of us in there. Remember, it was so crowded that I had to run the gear shift for you?"

Their laughter permeated deep into my aching heart, reaching memories and a cheerfulness I'd forgotten in my anguish.

Lisa added her own memory: "What about Sophomore

Skip Day when we snuck into Erica's house to go swimming?" Laughter burst out all over the room, bouncing off the walls.

"I got in so much trouble for that," Erica said. "The cleaning lady thought we were burglars. I found her hiding in the closet with the butcher knife." Another outburst of laughter cut her off. "If she'd had a phone she would have called the police. Thank goodness she recognized me and had a sense of humor."

They talked with me as though I responded, answered, and laughed along with their stories. I thought I had. It wasn't until much later that I found out I hadn't interacted at all. But the spike in my heart rate and flutter of my eyelids when they spoke led them to believe I could hear them. And I did. Their visit meant the world to me. They showed their love and support by bringing happiness with them. They offered themselves even when they were told it wouldn't make a difference, but it did. Laughter and happiness were mine for a short time. The four-hour drive wasn't an easy trip for them, but their willingness to bolster my spirits became a ray of light.

I needed an emotional boost because the next day I had to worry about the amputation of my left hand above the wrist and right ring finger, as well as the closure of my leg wounds. I was heading into deep water, where I would have to struggle to get back to shore.

As my bed was rolled down the hallway to the operating room, Scott kept a hand resting on my shoulder, as he always did on tough days. I was awake enough to know what was going to happen but not coherent enough to understand why.

"No. I don't want to go," I mumbled in his direction.

"I know. It will be okay," Scott said as he walked next to the bed.

I cried weakly as we reached the operating room doors. "I don't want them to . . . I don't want to go."

"I'll be here when you wake up. I love you."

Unable to comprehend the necessity of the surgery, I called to Scott and begged the doctors to let me go. Scott stood and watched them take me away. The guilt of letting them take another piece of his wife was overpowered by the hope of my survival. But that didn't stop his heart from aching at what I was about to lose.

The family and friends who showed up day after day created the foundation I needed to get through the amputations. Amputations brought many challenges—the most immediate and difficult to ignore being a constant ache and burning in my residuals (the medical term for my remaining limbs). It wasn't easy for my family to watch, but they came anyway. Not only did my family have to see me suffer, they had to explain what had happened over and over again.

My mother in particular struggled with what I had endured. Our already solid relationship was strengthened during my illness. When I was fourteen my parents separated, only to divorce a few years later. My mother and I drew close together during those years, splitting the responsibility of paying bills, cleaning, cooking, and grocery shopping. We took on home improvement projects like fixing sprinklers and painting the house. She was my confidant and friend. As a grown woman, I still called her when I was having a bad day. She would tell me to put on happy music and think of the good things in my life.

Listening to her voice gave me strength. I can only imagine her suffering as she watched what I went through.

While I was in the hospital, she and my brother Shawn came to be with me Friday through Monday. She adjusted her work schedule so she could provide tenderness and care in the way only a mother could. She put lip balm on my parched lips and brushed my hair away from my face.

Music had always had a powerful influence on my moods, so she brought a CD player with a variety of listening choices. At first nothing helped. Books on CD and music agitated me. Finally, she brought in a CD of water sounds. Running water, crashing waves, and pattering rain soothed my nerves and created a calm that flowed from my mind to the rest of my body.

When I couldn't stop tears from falling, she'd whisper, "You can do this. You're going to make it."

There were days I needed her like I needed air.

A few days after my hand and finger were amputated, she tugged at the ends of my fingertips, carefully clipping each nail. I didn't realize I was counting—one, two, three—until she missed the fourth finger and moved to my pinkie.

"Mom," I stopped her. "You missed one."

"No. I didn't," she replied, pulling away the last bit of nail.

"Yes, you did. I was counting. You missed my ring finger."

"What?" she asked, her confusion clouding the question.

"My ring finger, you missed it," I said again.

A stifled sob reached my ears. I hated when she cried, especially if I didn't understand why. It was only a missed fingernail. I tried to sit up, to reach out to her, but my body wouldn't obey. I managed to turn my head in her direction.

"Mom, what's wrong?"

"Scott said he told you."

"Told me what? What are you talking about?" Mentally scanning my memories, I tried to discover what I'd forgotten.

"Oh, Carol, he said you knew. I'm sorry. I'm so sorry."

My heart rate picked up. I had the feeling there was something important I should remember.

"Mom, just tell me." I tried to face her, to look into her eyes so I could see her fear and understand her distress. The image of her familiar face appeared so clearly before me I forgot I couldn't see.

Scott was always the first one to give me bad news. It was too hard for my mom to witness my first reactions. This time it couldn't be avoided. My blindness caused much of my confusion. I couldn't see my missing feet or hand. Large doses of medication dulled my senses enough that I couldn't tell my limbs weren't there. I only knew they hurt.

"Your finger was amputated in the last operation." The truth came tumbling out of her. "Your left hand, too. I thought you knew. I'm so sorry," she sobbed.

I sat in stunned silence, thinking. I couldn't have forgotten something like that, could I?

"Don't you remember the last operation?" she asked desperately.

"Oh, yeah," I said quietly under my breath. I tried to remember. Meanwhile, I pretended to know what she was talking about. Eerily, my own nightmares were often more real than the thought of my amputations, because I "saw" my nightmares with vivid detail. But, if I thought hard enough,

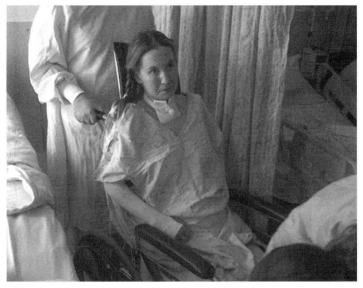

Learning to sit up in a wheelchair for respiratory therapy at the hospital.

there were memories hidden behind the power of medication and darkness of my eyes.

The dosage of my medication was reduced enough that memories started to come together, forming a horrifying picture. My left hand, a blood clot, they had to take it or infection could spread to the rest of my body. When conscious, I tried to process all that had happened, all that was lost, and what it meant for my future, but learning that those vague memories were real increased my physical and emotional torment.

My days were full of ups and downs that I was able to get through only with the persistence and determination of my family support system. The more I was conscious, the more I fought the anxiety caused by constant pain and continued hospitalization. My time at Swedish Medical Center was marked and punctuated by episodes of tearful conversations and anxiety attacks.

"Mom?" I called softly. A weak echo bounced off the walls, reaching nothing but the corners of my empty room.

"Mom!"

Fear coiled around my slowly constricting throat. How I wished I could move to escape the aching in my legs and the confines of the bed. My head started rocking, slowly at first, but as the fear pulled in tighter, my head moved faster. Moving back and forth, I couldn't stop calling for my mom. If I could focus on her, then maybe I could stop feeling.

"Mom!"

A nurse came into my room. "Can I get you something?"

"Mom?"

She hesitated. "Your mom isn't here."

"Where is she? I need her. Mom!" My swaying gained speed.

"Try to calm down. Can you take a deep breath for me?" She moved closer. I heard her adjust a monitor. "I think she just took a trip down the hall to get something to eat. I'm sure she'll be right back."

I tried to force air into my lungs, but my diaphragm shuddered like a hiccup. The fear wouldn't release me, and the piercing ache in my arm and legs wouldn't stop. I was trapped in my own body. Shallow, little breaths didn't provide enough oxygen as I was buried alive in my own fear. Shaking my head, my pleas continued, "Mom, Mom."

A worried sigh escaped the nurse. "I've already given you something for anxiety. I'll go find your mom. I'll be back."

"Yeah, okay." I calmed. My ears pricked up listening,

waiting for a sound that only my mom would make. I continued to quietly whisper for her as the world closed in around me.

"I found your mom," an excited nurse exclaimed as she threw open the door.

"Carol?"

"Mom!" I sobbed.

"Honey, what's wrong?" my mom asked, coming in close.

What's wrong? I thought. *I am wrong.* Everything was wrong. But I couldn't say that.

"Mom, these things on my legs hurt. Can you make them take them off? The things on my legs and whatever is on my ear."

"Take them. . . ." She and the nurses looked at the heavy machines attached to the ends of my legs. They kept suction on the wounds to keep the circulation going. A heart monitor was attached to my ear.

"We can't do that," said the nurse.

"They have to stay on," my mom said as a gentle reminder. "You won't get better without them."

"Please? Please—Mom." I broke down into whimpers and turned my head side to side. I didn't care about getting better.

"Mom. . . ." I muttered.

"Let's turn on your water CD," she said. Waves crashing on the beach drowned out my pleas for my mother. I sat back, hoping the waves could wash away everything. That panic attack lasted two days. With my mom's deeply-rooted strength that never wavered, she stayed with me, helplessly watching me suffer.

In a strange way, sepsis pulled my family together. I would

never have chosen trauma as a catalyst for change, but my illness brought me closer to many of the people in my life—Scott, Heath, Shawn, my mom, and my dad.

My brother Shawn came with my mom every weekend. He'd moved in with her a short time after my illness because he was fighting some addictions while going through a difficult divorce. Even under sedation, I worried about Shawn. My heart rate would rise when he entered the room. But his kind, personable nature put me at ease.

He was the guy in high school that everyone wanted to be. Tall and athletic, his "who-cares" attitude disguised the sensitive soul inside. He would come in close when he spoke to me. Had I been able to see, I'm sure he would have been too close for most people's comfort, but that's who he was.

He would stroke my hair when he spoke to let me know he was nearby. "Can I get you anything?"

I'd shake my head no.

He kissed my forehead before he continued. "I tell everyone about you, like what a great mom you are and how much you like to snowboard. I talked to Mike. Do you remember him from high school? I asked him to pray for you. He goes to church so he said he'd have the people at his church pray for you too."

"You don't need to do that." Sometimes I hated how much I'd changed everyone's lives.

Shawn ignored my protest and kept talking. Listening to his voice took me away from the hospital to better places. He kept me up to date on our old acquaintances and what was happening outside the hospital.

"Scott's awesome." He told me one day.

"I know," I said quietly.

"I was right about him."

My brow furrowed. "What do you mean you were right?"

"He's worth keeping around. I told you that when you were dating." I could almost hear the smirk in his voice.

Shawn had been my advisor when Scott and I were dating. "When we broke up that one time . . ." I paused to take a deep breath. " . . . you told me not to be the girl that called him right away. To give him some space."

"And did it work?"

It was too tiring to really argue with him. "Yes." I tried to hide my smile. "It worked."

"See. I was right." Shawn knew how and when to tease to lighten my mood.

After my parents divorced, my dad remained an important influence in my life, as well as that of my brothers, who have a different biological father—a distinction he and my brothers hardly ever made. However, he wasn't involved in my daily life. Over the years we had grown apart. My dad wouldn't go near a hospital for any reason, but when I became sick, he didn't run and hide or stay away. He marched back into my life with gusto.

"Carol Jean, it's Dad!" he would call as he threw open the door to my hospital room. "How are you doing today? It's as cold as a meat locker in here. How can you stand it?" I could hear the rustle of his windbreaker as he rubbed his arms for warmth. The smell of his cologne and coffee quickly filled the room. I couldn't help but smile when I thought of his Tom Selleck mustache and handsome face.

"Not cold to me."

Baby Safiya held lovingly by her grandfather, "Pops."

He and my stepmother, Judy, adjusted their full-time work schedules so they could be with me every Tuesday through Thursday. Judy always made a point to make a trip to the NICU to hold Safiya while I had visitors. I appreciated the thoughtfulness she showed Safiya when I couldn't hold her myself.

Given my dad's feelings about hospitals, his regular visits prompted a renewal of our relationship. Unbeknownst to me, my dad had heart problems at the time. A narrowing of his arteries required stents to be placed in his heart. When it came time for surgery, he asked that I not be told. He wanted me to focus on getting better.

My dad also became my coconspirator, bringing me the innocent contraband that everyone else, including the doctors, insisted I avoid.

"Don't tell anyone," he'd whisper, popping the top of a soda can. "It's Sprite." I probably shouldn't have had most of the things he brought me. But if I mentioned something in particular I wanted, the next time he came, he'd bring it.

With the support of my family, my recovery continued. In the meantime, Safiya grew strong, gained weight, and was ready to go home long before I was. Scott often told me how feisty she was. Her temper made her difficult to console, but her stubbornness helped her survive.

After five weeks at the hospital, Safiya was scheduled to go home. Scott asked the hospital to wait so he could make the necessary arrangements. Caring for a five-week-old preemie, an eighteen-month-old, a disabled wife, and his dental business was more than he could manage on his own. He put the word out to friends and family that he quickly needed to find someone with medical training. This person needed to be willing to take care of the girls and, later, me.

Erin Stout was recommended by a close family friend. During her career as an LPN, she'd worked in nursing homes and with disabled children. When she retired, she told her family to hit her over the head with a frying pan if she ever tried to go back to work.

Scott first interviewed her at our home. She later told me that when she walked inside the nursery, it seemed as though I had just stepped out for a moment. The nesting instinct had kicked in months before my due date, so Safiya's room was perfectly arranged with the clothes prewashed and neatly folded in the drawers. Toys were put away in coordinating bins, and the matching curtains and crib accessories were in place. Everything in that room was organized exactly as it had been the day I went to the hospital.

Scott was ready to hire her right away, but when Erin saw

the thoughtful way I'd organized the nursery, she insisted on meeting me before the contract was signed. She said, "Anyone with a home that organized should approve of the person who will be caring for her."

When we met, I explained Chloe's daily routine down to the minutest detail. How long breakfast lasted, what she ate for snacks, and that she only watched one video after lunch. It had been almost three months since I'd cared for Chloe, but Erin listened attentively and said, "I think I can manage that."

Erin wanted to know how *I* wanted things done. She never imposed her own preferences, instead choosing to discipline and arrange days the way I would. With six grown children of her own, I'm sure she had different ideas than I did, but she followed my routine and ran the house as I saw fit. It helped me trust her right away. She deferred to me as mother rather than insisting she, with her experience, knew best.

After meeting us and observing our situation, she told her family, "You're going to have to hit me with a frying pan, because I'm going to work for this family. They need me, and I think I can help." She immediately took the job.

I will always think of Erin as "Nanny." That's what the girls and I called her. She brought them to visit me at the hospital and would prove to be an angel in disguise.

With the girls taken care of, I prepared for the next step in my recovery. Because of the support I had, I was ready. There was hope and confidence knowing I had loyal people who kept me from falling too deep into the tides of sepsis. Through their support, I felt a strengthening love that gave me hope of my own and motivation to try.

CHAPTER 6

❧

Into the Dark

"It can be said that living without hope is like no longer living. Hell is hopelessness, and it is not for nothing that at the entrance to Dante's hell there stand the words: 'Abandon all hope, ye who enter here.'"
—Jürgen Moltmann

Forty-nine days.

That's how long it had been since my life had changed forever. Forty-nine days of confusion, pain, fear, and shock. Forty-nine tear-filled days, the worst of my life. I was ready to leave, to move on to something better, easier, happier, brighter.

Scott had done his research and chose to move me from Swedish Medical Center to Harborview, one of the best medical facilities in the Seattle area for skin grafts. Harborview was the first step past survival toward recovery.

As we readied to leave Swedish, my emotions ranged from sadness at leaving the staff I'd come to trust to excitement at the idea of starting the recovery process. After tearful goodbyes to the staff and therapists, I lay in bed, listening to the bustling sounds of change. Scott talked to the nurse about paperwork while my in-laws packed my cards, flowers, and chocolates.

I could hear my mother-in-law, Joanne, gathering cards near my bed. Guilt swept over me, as it often did when she was in the room. Because of me, she had to watch her son suffer. Because of me, her life would never be the same. I longed to see her face. Was she angry? Tired? Did she wish I weren't there?

"I'm so sorry," I said, fighting back tears. "I'm sorry this happened."

Joanne's movement stopped. Gently her hands grasped either side of my face, and with a sincerity born of love, she said, "Don't you do that. This is not your fault."

I needed that reassurance, but, to my surprise, I didn't believe her. Even if *she* didn't blame me, guilt had anchored itself too deeply.

After waiting all day for the ambulance transport to take me to Harborview, the medics' deep voices drifted into my room. Their presence solidified the reality of the coming move. It was time to go. My heart pounded as I listened to the gurney rattle into the room.

"We're going to slide you onto a board and then lift you onto the gurney. Are you ready?"

I nodded.

Their movements were slow and smooth, as though I weighed nothing. The gurney felt different from my hospital bed—elevated, stiff, restrained. Straps tightened around my legs and abdomen, confining me in a way I wasn't used to. I wondered how rough of a ride they expected. They wheeled the gurney through the hospital exit, and I took in my first breath of fresh air in nearly two months. Instinctively I looked to the sky, but I saw nothing through my darkened eyes.

The cool, crisp evening breeze was full of possibilities as I let it fill my lungs. I heard the sounds of the city—honking horns, rumbling engines, shoes tapping, laughing voices. Sound moved differently outside as it bounced off buildings and collided with the movement of the humid air, freely scattering in all directions. As they lifted the gurney into the ambulance, I felt as though an adventure was about to begin.

The ambulance moved with a sluggish, exaggerated sway. The ride to Harborview was a symphony of familiar but newly meaningful sounds: the rattle of the medical supplies, the squeak of the brakes, the growl of the engine, the hum of the medics, and finally, the click of the door latch as it opened. I silently said goodbye to the fresh air as they wheeled me inside the hospital.

A loud, vivacious voice welcomed me. "Don't you worry about a thing, darlin'. We're gonna take good care of you." The familiar squeak and pull of wheels turning over linoleum brought the owner of the voice, a woman, closer. She talked me through check-in with words so full of confidence I couldn't help but believe her.

The medical team at Harborview didn't waste time. As soon as Scott and I settled into my room, the doctor assessed my case and dropped hope-crushing information. "To prevent infection, we'll need to cap the trach tube before we can do a full assessment. You'll have to be under full sedation to lessen the pain. The trach tube will need to remain closed for the duration of the skin graft procedures."

"No!" I cried without thinking. The doctor didn't know

it, but he'd pronounced a death sentence. Complete separation and isolation from the world around me—that's death. Without my eyes, words had become the only way I could interact with the world. With the trach tube capped, I wouldn't be able to talk or communicate. My wants, needs, and worries would be mine alone. All my anticipation and excitement were swept away. Then the words "methadone" and "standard procedure" drifted to my ears. When I'd been at Swedish, methadone had caused nightmares so terrifying I had refused to take it, but that wasn't an option at Harborview. A knot crept into my stomach as I realized recovery meant sinking into an ever-darkening abyss.

How I felt didn't matter. It was necessary, and I knew it.

Before long, I found myself lying on a bed pushed against the wall in what sounded like an expansive, isolated hallway. I waited alone, afraid. I heard the occasional echoes of a distant door opening and closing and wondered if the doctors and nurses had lost or forgotten me. Tears trickled down my cheeks, slowly making their way onto the pillow. I didn't have the ability to wipe them from my own face.

Finally, someone came. My bed shook as they rolled me into the operating room, where I was given medication that dulled my senses. Soon all sound stopped. No beeps from the machines, or hum of electricity, or even the rustle of the scrubs worn by the doctors. The beating of my heart pulsated loudly in my ears. I was trapped in a world of my own half-formed thoughts, drifting in the growing darkness of my mind. I couldn't see. I couldn't speak. I couldn't move. I floated alone in a darkness devoid of life, light, and feeling. There was nothing left but to submit, give in to the drugs, and sink into the suffocating void.

So began a miserable, sorrow-filled ten days while the trach cap was in place; time flowed together, never separating into day or night. For me, time wasn't measured by days or weeks. I lived by moments. Moments of deep, frightening confusion as all the major skin grafts I needed to survive took place.

I would not wish a skin graft on my worst enemy.

Skin grafting is a medical marvel, but it's a horrifying experience. Because of the severity of my case, I needed full-thickness grafts all over my body. Full-thickness grafts not only take the top two layers of skin, as split-thickness grafts do, but some muscle and blood vessels as well. Nerves are left exposed as skin is harvested to later be sewn in place, piece by piece. Before my skin was literally peeled from my body, they did grafts with cadaver skin to be sure my body would accept a graft at all.

After this initial success, they scraped a layer of skin from my back, extending from the bottom of my scapula to my hips. Once removed, the skin was rolled out in a mesher. It made tiny cuts in the skin so that it could be thinned and stretched for maximum coverage. They reattached it to my legs, arms, and parts of my abdomen. I became a patchwork doll stitched together with dark purple areas mixed with islands of my natural pink skin.

As horrible as the skin grafts were, nothing could have prepared me for the torture of dressing changes, which were done frequently to prevent infection.

Each time, the voices of three or four nurses and staff echoed in a quiet, stale room. They talked me through each step in a vain effort to alleviate my fear. Their words were kind and gentle, but what they *said* was in stark contrast to what they *did*. Their voices stayed soft as they peeled away the dressings, trying to protect the tender new layers of skin on my body. They were kind and compassionate, but it felt as though I were skinned alive over and over again. I wanted to scream, but I couldn't. With my trach tube capped, screams came out as tortured moans.

They worked quickly, methodically moving through my back, arms, legs, and stomach. Just when I thought they were done, they'd move to another area of my body.

"Suck on your lollipop, Carol," they'd say as my moans grew louder.

The lollipop laced with painkillers didn't help the pain so much as give me something else to focus on. I sucked on it, trying to block out the pulling and burning sensations. I didn't know one person could endure such torture. I survived, but I will never forget how it felt. Dressing changes became a regular part of my life. I went to dark places in my mind, trying to escape. However, the only escape was to endure each dressing change one at a time.

Harborview had a policy requiring methadone for grafts and dressing changes. I suppose it suppressed the pain to a degree, although I wouldn't have thought it at the time. It was meant to help me, but it had a dreadful side effect. Without my eyes to give all the sounds, smells, and textures meaning, my brain tried to make order of the world but failed miserably. My drugged mind conjured scenarios and hallucinations that challenged what I knew to be true. Those unlikely scenarios became my reality. Sometimes I thought I was in a homeless shelter lying on a mattress on the floor, only to discover I was in a

POW camp with vials and machinery clanking around me. I couldn't understand why I was there or what was happening. At the time, I was sure it was all real.

I struggled to remain calm, to stay in touch with the real world. My mom played my water CDs. The sound of rain drowned out the chaos created by my mind. When I wasn't terrorized by hallucinations, I struggled to come to terms with my illness and the extent of my injuries. Between the medications and my mixed-up senses, the dark thoughts that had stalked me since the beginning of my illness—guilt and despair—began to seize control. As a protection, I tried to shut down my emotions, numbing myself.

I pushed everything out. Even hope.

I didn't die, but I ceased to live.

I merely existed as a person floating alone on a stormy sea. Waves of agony from the mental and physical trauma crashed over me until I thought I would drown. Many times I screamed inside, but no one could hear. Drugs and pain often left me nauseous and vomiting. I would come up, gasping for air, yearning for the slightest chance of rescue or reprieve.

I reached out to whomever I could find. The touch of Scott holding my hand, Heath stroking my hair, or sometimes a kind word from a compassionate nurse would be enough to pull me through until the next wave of agony began. My world became a cycle of agonized awakenings followed by a struggle to escape in sleep. I was devoid of all but the most tormented emotions.

The rigorous schedule of procedures and surgeries took its toll. My body rebelled. As I awakened from anesthesia, uncontrollable tremors shook my shrunken frame. The doctors prescribed more medications to stop the side effects of the drugs I needed to survive. The body can take only so much before it begins to collapse in on itself from the stress.

My situation became more complicated when I contracted MRSA, a drug-resistant bacterial infection. With my compromised immune system, it wasn't completely unexpected, but it was serious enough that it could have killed me. No one told me about the infection until much later. But I noticed doctors, nurses, and visitors began to scrub up and put on gowns and masks before they entered my room. All my procedures and daily care became more difficult in an attempt to keep the infection from taking my life and prevent it from spreading to other patients.

I had no control over my body or mind. That loss of power was more difficult than anything I had ever experienced. No part of me felt safe. For ten days, I was in and out of consciousness, trapped in a living nightmare.

At the end of the ten days, my new trach tube was opened. It was a brief glimmer of hope that was short-lived. The new trach tube was small and had to be plugged manually before I could speak. I couldn't plug it myself, so I had to coordinate my breathing with whomever I spoke to.

"How are you feeling?" Scott asked. He reached over and plugged the trach tube, which caused me to gasp and stutter. I tried again, desperate to get out a single word. More gasping and wheezing was followed by yet another attempt. All my mental and physical energy focused on speaking a single word, only to have it strangled by my inability to time my breathing. Exhausted from the effort, I lay back in defeat. Shaking my head no, I closed my eyes and sank into a restless sleep.

The forced silence I endured during the grafting process left me emotionally fragile. But the difficulty of speaking after the trach tube was opened pushed me too far. I stopped trying to talk altogether. Sleep was my escape, my one luxury; the only place I felt safe. At the time, I couldn't imagine how my life could get any more miserable. What little hope I still had was barely perceptible.

Basic physical therapy was started, with the goal of sending me home in a few months. I underwent respiratory therapy to learn how to sit up and breathe again.

"I want you to sit up. Place your arm down on the bed and roll toward it," the therapist would say. Then she'd wait.

Laying my arm on the bed was the only part of the whole process I managed with ease. "Now try to push up."

I pushed with all my strength, but nothing happened.

"Keep trying."

Gritting my teeth, I pushed harder and felt my body move slightly.

"Good." Her hands grasped my body, pulling me up the rest of the way.

My muscles quivered. Every day the therapist came, and we'd do it again.

A few days later, a wrist cuff with a spoon attached was strapped to my wrist. Two unsuccessful bites later, I was too tired to lift my arm.

After six weeks, the doctors and my family had a meeting to decide how to proceed. I was there too but was under such heavy medication I couldn't participate in the discussion. Reviewing the facts of my case and my eligibility for an at-home rehab program called Rehab Without Walls, it was decided to send me home.

I had made good physical progress. However, there were some significant milestones that had to be met before I would be ready to leave.

Complicating the situation was another serious but less dangerous infection in my back, pushing my release date out another week. My mom and Erin had to learn to shower me and correctly care for the infection on my back and wounds on my hips, which had yet to heal properly. Showers left me in tears and screaming. Erin and my mom watched, studying how to do it themselves. I couldn't bear the thought of my mom seeing me in that condition. I begged her to leave, but she refused. She stayed, watched, and learned, understanding that proper care was critical to successfully bringing me home.

Getting approval proved to be the easiest step to getting out of the hospital. For two and a half months I'd had a catheter in place to remove urine from my bladder. Periodically, the catheter was taken out and replaced with a bed pan or diapers. Within a week of the decision to send me home, I learned to sit up in bed, which meant I could sit on a toilet. I was scheduled to leave the next day, but my body didn't follow my brain's commands.

I sat and sat. Finally, I looked to the nurse and my mom. "What should I do? Nothing is happening."

A brilliant idea struck my mom. "When you were a little girl I used to turn the faucet on to get you to go. That's how I potty trained you."

"Let's do it then and get this over with," I said. We turned the faucet on and, as it turns out, it had the same effect as it had when I was a little girl.

Home had been my goal for so long that it felt surreal. I yearned for the welcome, safety, and warmth of familiar surroundings and grew excited once the decision was made. I would get back to my life, my girls, and my own bed. I would be me again. I didn't know then that things would get worse in the one place I never expected it.

When release day finally came, zippers, bags, plastic, and the sounds of fabric being folded filled my room. Specialists with instructions and goodbyes and nurses offering comfort and encouragement were music to my ears. I was going home! Hope, which had been so elusive, began to grow, but underneath I fought an unexpected fear. My life had been full of pain managed by the hospital staff. Could Scott, my mom, or anyone help me keep it under control? I pushed fear and doubt down into a dark corner where it stayed away from the surface. But anxiety had a way of bubbling up, making my optimism and hope waver.

I fought against it with good humor. When I was transferred from my hospital bed to a wheelchair, I joked with my brothers and the nurses. For the time being, the pain was under control, but the dosage would slowly decrease over the next three days.

The mood shifted as I was wheeled out of the hospital. The world expanded in all directions. I became aware of my own insignificance and vulnerability. Without the secure walls of the hospital, I didn't know how to trust anyone or anything. As we neared the crosswalk, I could hear cars driving by. To me, they sounded like they were speeding on an interstate.

"Are the cars going to hit us?" I asked, surprised by my reaction.

"No. We're all clear," the nurse answered as she started to push me into the crosswalk.

I didn't believe her. The cars sounded so close. "Wait. Are you sure? Did you check both ways?"

"Yes. We can cross."

I pushed myself deep into the seat of the wheelchair, bracing for the impact of a moving vehicle. Shaking with terror, I tried to keep from asking again if there were cars coming. I could hear them, but I didn't know how close they were. I hadn't learned to use sound to gauge distance. I was breathing heavily before we reached the other side.

We made it to the car safely, only to discover yet another problem: I'd lost so much weight I didn't fit in the front seat. Scott and Heath placed pillows at my feet and sides, as my legs could no longer reach the ground to support my body. After I got adjusted, Scott buckled my seat belt and we were on our way.

It was a rough hour-long ride, even with the pillows. I slid and flopped while trying to steady myself without a working hand. I was used to sitting upright in a hospital bed or wheelchair, not a moving vehicle. Scott reached his arm across my body to help, but there was little he could do. Though I still had pain medication in my system from the hospital, the aching began to creep its way past the drugs. I moaned and whimpered as I tried to stay upright in the seat. I felt like a rag doll helplessly thrown with every bump and turn. To make matters worse, as we neared my house, I had to use the bathroom.

As Scott scooped me out of the seat and ran into the

Me and Erin Stout, aka "Nanny."

house, I was horrified and humiliated realizing that my husband would have to help me go to the bathroom. But he did, without reservation or judgment. Then he carried me to rest in our bed. Relaxing in my own home, in my own bed, was something I'd dreamed about for weeks. My bed represented the comfort I'd been missing for months. It was a return to normalcy, a return to *my* life.

But my bed betrayed me.

A thin sheen of sweat broke out on my forehead. My aching body yearned for relief, but my bed wasn't soft and welcoming like the warm embrace I remembered. It wasn't a place I could melt into and feel safe. The weight of the down comforter made my skin grafts hurt, and the sheets bound around me. Pain was everywhere, and I couldn't stop it.

I tried to adjust my position, but my weakened body felt thick and heavy. After months of being in a hospital bed, I couldn't do it on my own. Scott tried to prop me up with pillows or turn me on my side, but I couldn't get comfortable. Gauze encased my abdomen, trapping the heat against my body. All of my residuals were covered with gauze and an additional layer of a special compression fabric, which meant more heat. As the heat built, so did my worry. Scott turned on the ceiling fan, which offered some relief but not enough.

Home was supposed to make me feel better, not worse. Lying there, disappointment and doubt flooded through me. *How could I have thought this would work?* I couldn't even lie in my own bed. I needed help with everything. At the hospital, it seemed natural to need help—expected. The nurses were paid to take care of me. Here, Erin was paid, but everyone else was a person I loved and cared for. I felt I'd become a burden with nothing of value to offer. They had lives and responsibilities. Anxiety began to feed on itself, growing larger until it turned to panic. A harsh reality set in, and I knew I couldn't stay.

My voice and body shook as I spoke. "You need to take me back. I want to go back to the hospital."

"No, Carol," Scott calmly replied.

"I don't belong here. You shouldn't have to do this. I should be in a nursing home."

"I can take care of you," he said with a confidence I didn't have.

When reason didn't work, I begged.

"Please take me back," I desperately pleaded. "I want to go back!"

"This is where you belong. We can do this," Scott said with a firm but gentle assurance.

I loved him for his optimism, but I knew I didn't belong

At home in my bed holding Safiya.

at home. There were so many things that could hurt or even kill me. What would I do without sponge baths, professional bandage changes, a therapeutic bed, and a full dose of painkillers? The hospital was where I belonged, where I felt safe. Scott wouldn't give in.

How could he not understand? I was sure someone must have led us astray. This wasn't supposed to be my life. I lay with my body aching and sweat building as the challenges I faced and difficulties that lay ahead sunk in all at once. Around me, people shuffled packages, shut drawers, and someone was setting up a bedside commode all in a place that should be my sanctuary. A cold awareness spread through me as I realized my old life was gone. If I couldn't have my old life, what kind of life could I have? If I *were* in the right place, it shouldn't be this hard.

"Take me back, please!" I pleaded again. "I have to go back."

"No, Carol. I can take care of you," replied Scott firmly. "You belong here. We're going to figure this out."

I wanted to believe him, but everything around me suggested otherwise. Two hours after I arrived home, complications arose. The hole left by the trach tube kept opening when I tried to swallow my medication, which meant pain was building without relief. We called the doctor, whose solution was simple: use a straw. My trouble taking the pills was a pattern for all that was to come. I needed a solution for everything from eating to showering to sitting in a chair. In many ways, I felt like a newborn child, completely dependent on those around me.

I hated it.

Rather than getting better at home, I entered a downward spiral fed by frustration, longing, anger, and an overwhelming despair. Hope was gone.

Every day our home was full of people—family, friends, neighbors, therapists.

My family rented a house nearby to give them all a place to stay when they traveled from elsewhere. Shawn moved permanently into the rental house and began looking for a job. He wanted to be nearby to help during my recovery, and he hoped that by leaving the place where his addictions had started he would be able to break the cycle.

Everyone's emotions ran high from the moment I woke in the morning until I tried to get comfortable at night. I cried while I screamed or yelled. Other times, tears slid silently down my cheeks as Shawn or Heath knelt at my bedside wiping them away. Chaotic outbursts and arguments were common. I would get upset about my situation and someone would say, "We can't go there," while someone else argued, "If she wants to talk, let her talk!"

When a therapist from the Department of Services for the Blind showed up, I couldn't face her. She tried to show me how I could label my cupboards. I couldn't even sit in a chair at the time. I told Scott, "I don't want her here. I don't need her help." I had so many other problems that learning to live as a blind person seemed far down on my list of concerns. I assumed my eyesight would return in the future. My family disagreed, but I insisted.

We argued about the girls, my treatment plan, and other less important things. My need to talk about my condition led to arguments with Scott, my mom, Heath, and everyone else in the room. Emotions crackled like static electricity, ready to spark at the slightest movement. We were all trying to cope with our feelings and the trials of my illness, which made for a tense situation.

Fear consumed me. I *knew* I couldn't do it, but everyone around me kept pretending that things would get better. *Is this really the life I want?* I asked myself. At the hospital, I could control my fear, escaping in sleep, but at home, fear ran rampant—fear of pain, fear of what I couldn't see, fear of the future. And fear of myself.

I became edgy, doubtful, and a victim. I always assumed the worst would happen to me, and many times, it did. Nothing was easy. I felt like a helpless child when my mom and Erin changed my bandages, moving me around like a ninety-pound infant. It was humiliating. The entire process

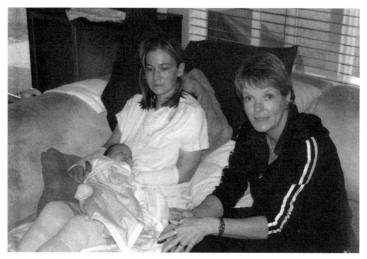

Holding Safiya with my stepmother, Judy, next to me.

of showering, bandaging, and getting dressed took two hours, leaving me exhausted.

But that wasn't the most miserable part of being home. Chloe, my little girl I had never left for a day of her life before my illness, was afraid of me. She was my world. Her fear cut at the most tender parts of my heart and identity as a mother. Every morning I could hear Shawn playing with her. He would talk in his Donald Duck voice while she giggled uncontrollably. I hated that he could make her laugh and I couldn't. I hated that I hated when anyone could do the things I couldn't.

And Safiya—I had yet to truly bond with her, although I tried.

Holding her was a monumental task. Propped up, with a pillow over my sensitive leg grafts, I couldn't wait to feel her soft little body. But when I held her, I felt nothing. With little sensitivity in my remaining hand, I couldn't feel the warmth of her body or smoothness of her skin. Holding her on my lap was awkward at best and excruciating at worst. Touching my grafts, even with a gentle fingertip through my clothing, sent searing waves through my body. Holding a squirming infant was unbearable. I could hold her for only a few minutes at a time.

My heart broke.

Someone else held, fed, washed, and dressed my baby. I couldn't even remember giving birth to her. Somehow, I lost that sense of her and me belonging to one another. I'd missed the important moments mothers share with their newborns. I wondered if I would ever feel that attachment. Other people got to love Safiya and Chloe while I was in another room enduring my personal torture. Other people—not me—played with and cared for my daughters, doing my job. How could I be a mom again? How could I be anything? A wife? A daughter? A friend?

With my body and heart broken, my spirit broke, too. I shut down as a way to protect myself from the emotional wounds. My anguish paved the way for anger. I lashed out at my family about Erin or anyone else caring for the girls. I wanted my daughters to have everything they wanted, whether it was good for them or not. At one point, I even wanted Erin gone. I resented her. She was doing the job that should have been mine.

Though my mom offered wise counsel—"No one will ever love your children the way you do. They need you"—I wasn't able to believe her. I couldn't see how they could possibly need me.

Thrown into the chaotic mix was newly emerging phantom

pain in my legs and left arm. My new doses of medication couldn't stop the burning sensation. I would raise my arms in the air and try to shake off a fire that wasn't there. My feeble attempts didn't last long, as they took all of what little energy I had. Some of the problems lay in learning how to manage my pain correctly. Timing the medication was key, and Erin made sure everyone understood what needed to be done so my pain level didn't get too high. But the learning curve was steep, and my anxiety and anger skyrocketed.

My lack of trust in my own body and the people around me triggered big outbursts at small annoyances. The volume on the TV, the girls' laughter, or the clothes I wore could be enough to set me off. I lashed out at the things I could change, but the source of my anguish came from the things that were out of my control: my physical pain, of course, but also everything else that reminded me I wasn't the person I used to be.

Mercifully, hope would occasionally peek through my misery. Handling our medical bills for my three months of care in the hospital was a serious concern for Scott and me. Two nurses from the town in which we lived hosted an auction-style fundraiser to help pay for medical bills. They weren't friends or family or even friends *of* family. They were strangers. Enumclaw is a small town of just over 11,500 people. Five thousand people showed up for the fund-raiser—most of them were strangers too.

I was asked to attend. All I wanted to do was stay home and wallow in misery. I didn't want people to see me as some kind of freak show. Somehow, Scott convinced me to go. My mom helped fix my hair, put makeup on me, and bought new clothes for me. It made me feel a little better. I didn't know what to expect as Shawn pushed my wheelchair through the

Thousands of Enumclaw community members came together, showing support by raising funds for my medical expenses.

auditorium doors, but I never imagined applause. Loud, reverberating, vibrating applause . . . for *me*. It was deafening as it rumbled in my chest. I could *feel* the crowd's love and concern. Warmth, friendship, and hope emanated from those good people, cutting through the heavy blanket of my emotions.

I didn't try to stop my tears. I couldn't believe it. I was nobody. Why would they do this for me? Strangers sacrificed their time and money to help me, when I was no more special than anyone else in the room. Their innate need to lessen my suffering was a balm to my weary soul. It buoyed me for a while, giving me space and time to feel joy. But after the applause died down and the evening was over, the hopelessness I felt deep inside remained. I could vaguely hear their message of hope, but I was too far into the darkness.

Try as I might, I couldn't hold on to the love and comfort

of that evening or any of the other small moments of happiness I experienced. The only things I knew were pain, loss, and the echoes of my own dark thoughts.

The darkness culminated one morning when I was home alone with Shawn and Erin. I hadn't been feeling well, and I was caught in a running loop of all the things I couldn't do, things I couldn't be. I couldn't see the faces of my little girls. I couldn't walk or run with them. I didn't know who I was. I would never be independent. Literally and figuratively, I couldn't see a way out of my worthless life.

Shawn was about to step outside when he asked me if I needed anything. At first I didn't answer, numbed by the questions that ran through my brain: *Where did I go wrong? What did I do to deserve this? Why me?* I'd had enough. I had reached the point of no return, past feeling. I was sure everyone's life would be easier without me, including my own.

Then I knew what I had to do. I stopped fighting the darkness. I refused to stay any longer and didn't want to pull my family into my despair anymore. I took control in the only viable way I could imagine. Numb and devoid of emotion I said, "Yes."

"What can I get you?" He asked as he gently touched my shoulder.

I looked up toward where I thought his face would be. "Shawn," I said, "you can get me a gun."

His clothing rustled as he came around the couch, standing close enough that his cologne filled my nostrils and I could feel his presence. His strong hands cupped each side of my face, hands that I knew and loved and trusted.

"Carol, we're not gonna go there," he said firmly. He sat

next to me and waited. In the silence was his concern and my despair.

"I couldn't kill myself if I wanted," I finally told him. "I can't hold a gun or pull a trigger. I've thought of taking too many pills, but I couldn't get them in my mouth by myself."

"We *are* going to get you through this, whatever it takes." Shawn kissed my forehead and stayed with me. No gun, no reprimand, no judgment.

I was in an empty, hopeless mental place that was so dark it sucked out life like a black hole. While I felt alone, I never was. Shawn, Heath, my parents, Scott's parents, Scott, and my beautiful babies were there. I couldn't yet fathom where their faith in me and my ability to heal came from.

Shawn's care and concern provided hope when I had none. He, like the rest of my family, loved me no matter my physical or emotional condition. I didn't realize it at the time, but I was at a turning point. Pieces of my life were about to slowly come back together. A moment of the grimmest despair passed through me. I wasn't out of the darkness yet, but I was preparing to take my first steps away from it.

CHAPTER 7

Surrendering with Blind Faith

"Faithless is he that says farewell when the road darkens."
—*J. R. R. Tolkien*

The darkness hadn't swallowed me completely, but I didn't know how to escape it. Two weeks after I went home, I had an appointment with Dr. Friedly, my rehabilitation doctor, to check on my progress. It came at the end of a long day that started with an appointment in the burn unit followed by a visit to a hand therapist. The paper on the exam table crinkled as I shifted, trying to get comfortable. After such a long day, it felt good to lie down.

Dr. Friedly examined my grafts and tested my muscle strength with little small talk. She hadn't said much before quietly leaving the room to check something. I lay silently as the nurse rewrapped my legs. The door opened and Dr. Friedly jumped right to the point. "The grafts are healing nicely and your muscle tone is getting better. In fact, you've made enough progress I think you're ready to start rehab anytime. I called the rehab center and they have an opening. It's yours if you want it."

I didn't respond.

"Well—" my mom spoke up next to me. "How long would we have to wait if she doesn't go now?"

"It could be another three or four months before a bed opens. Physically, I think you're ready. You'll need to let me know what you want to do within the next twenty-four hours. After that they'll give the bed to someone else." She grasped the door handle and turned back. "Think about it."

We weighed the pros and cons for the rest of the day.

"What do you think I should do?" I asked Scott late that night.

He laid my thin polar fleece blanket, the only cover I needed at night, over me before lying on the bed himself. The ceiling fan blew cool air over my body while my legs were motionless in leg immobilizers that kept my muscles extended while I slept. My right hand was stretched open in a brace.

Scott let out a heavy sigh. "You're going to have to go at some point. Why not now?"

I began to cry, as I often did. "But I just came home. I won't know anyone, and I'll have to be alone at night."

"Being at home hasn't been easy. At the hospital there won't be as many distractions, and you can focus on getting better. Dr. Friedly said that one day of inpatient rehab could do as much as three days of rehab at home."

I couldn't answer due to the tears. Coming home had brought nothing but a firm reminder of all I couldn't do— walk, hold Safiya, play with Chloe, cook meals. I couldn't take care of my own personal hygiene. I couldn't contribute to my family in any way. Knowing Dr. Friedly thought I was ready gave me a small seed of hope. Despite all my doubts, the idea was planted.

Scott wiped the tears from my face. "Maybe this is what you need. Harborview is one of the top four rehab programs in the country. I think you should go."

"So does everyone else." We'd had a long discussion when we'd gotten home with everyone in the family. I was the last holdout and, in a way, it was good that the decision was ultimately mine to make. I whispered, "What if I can't do it?"

"You won't know until you try. You can do it. I know you can. You'll still have weekends at home. Let's rest on it. Think about it overnight, and we'll decide in the morning."

"Okay." The possibilities played out in my mind until I couldn't hold sleep off any longer.

Rest provided the clarity I sought. Going through the laborious morning routine with Erin and my mom solidified what I'd already known: I needed rehab. Inpatient programs develop independence through the skills, strength, and coordination that can be achieved only with an intense daily regimen. I may not have wanted the rehab program, but I craved independence. I put aside doubt in the hope that something better awaited me. When I told Scott my decision, he made the call and started packing.

I would check into rehab the next day. The change and unknown brought fear and anxiety, clouding my ability to focus.

"I think we've got all the basics," said Scott as he zipped my suitcase.

My mom stepped in, pulling off my polar fleece blanket.

"Don't you want to take your blanket?" Leave it to my mom to sense my need for comfort.

I worried I might look silly bringing a security blanket to the hospital. My pride was squashed by the thought of sleeping alone at night. The blanket was coming. "Yes, I want it." My voice quivered. "Do you think I'll need anything else?"

Scott read off the checklist. I tried to visualize the items on the list, but he read so fast I lost track. I'd have to trust that he had everything.

"If you do need anything, I can bring it to you. We're only an hour away." He kissed my cheek.

Driving to the hospital that night, worries blocked reason: *What would they ask me to do? What if the pain was too much? What if I failed?* The questions rang through my head like fire alarms signaling me to get out. The hour-long drive to Seattle passed far too quickly. By the time Scott pushed my wheelchair into my private hospital room, I wanted him to turn around and take me home.

"This is a nice room, Carol." My mom circled the new space. "You've got some drawers here next to your bed, and a closet. There's a window to let in light. Isn't it nice that you have it all to yourself?"

"Yeah." A private room offered a small bit of peace.

Heath and Shawn unpacked my things while Scott laid me on the bed and put the polar fleece over me. They kept a running dialogue of what they were doing, but I wasn't listening. I didn't really care where my clothes were; I just wanted my family to stay. But, finally, everything was put away, and it was getting late.

"I think we're done here." Scott surveyed the room,

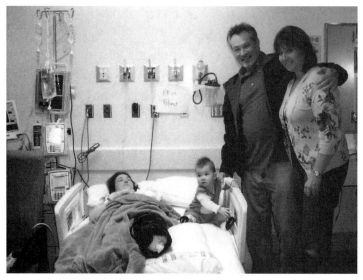

At rehab during a visit from my dad and Aunt Wendy.

meticulously checking each drawer. "It's time for us to go." I could hear him wiping down every surface with hand sanitizer. After so many infections the last time I was in the hospital, he'd become a little paranoid.

The panic I'd been holding in started to escape. "Not yet."

"He's right. It's time," Shawn conceded. "You need your rest. You have a big day tomorrow."

"No. . . ." I whimpered. I didn't want to be alone. All I would be left with were my thoughts and strangers I couldn't see. What if someone snuck into my room?

My mother brushed wisps of hair away from my face, tucking them behind my ear. "You're safe here. They'll take good care of you. I love you."

"Don't worry," Heath interjected. "I'll be back in the morning. Don't give them too much trouble tonight."

One by one they said their goodbyes—my mom with a touch on my cheek and Heath a squeeze to the shoulder.

Shawn left a kiss on my forehead with a hand on either side of my face. "I have to go back to the tri-cities to clear a few things in the divorce. I'll be back on the weekend." As much as I wanted him there, I was proud that he was working so hard to get his life straightened out.

The last was Scott. "I'll call you tomorrow. I love you." With a last kiss, I felt his presence move farther away as he joined the others. I listened to their footsteps fade out of the room and down the hallway.

My hearing stretched, reaching to stay with their familiar sounds as long as possible. Heath stopped the night nurse. "Take good care of her."

I cried alone.

Everything was strange—the sounds, the smells, the people. Rehab wasn't like the ICU or the burn unit. Taking shallow breaths, I listened to the deafening silence, afraid of what might happen during the night. The nurse came in to give me meds and show me how to use the call button.

During the night, my eyes popped open. I listened, trying to remember where I was. It wasn't home. Bumping my elbow on bed rails and smelling the unnaturally sterilized air gave it away. The hospital—rehab.

An urgency to use the bathroom caused me to fumble for the call button. With my right hand in a brace, all I had was my left arm residual, which was wrapped in bandages. I pressed what I thought was the call button over and over. But the bandage prevented any kind of sensation. I could have been pressing anything. Even if I'd had my bedside commode, I wouldn't have been able to get on it myself. When warmth filled my bed, my face burned in humiliation. I don't know how long I lay there before a nurse came in. The sound of the door opening brought relief and shame.

"Hello?" I called.

A deep voice answered, "Good morning."

Of course, it had to be a man, deepening my embarrassment.

"I've had an accident. I tried pressing the call button but no one came." It was hard to keep the accusation out of my voice. He came to my bed and found the button.

"I'm sorry. You were pressing the wrong side. We'll get you all cleaned up. Don't worry."

I tried not to bristle at his words. How was I supposed to not worry when I couldn't go to the bathroom by myself?

Heath arrived right after they'd gotten everything cleaned up. When he walked into my room I exclaimed, "Heath, I peed the bed on the first night. How am I ever going to do this?" Learning to function with disabilities meant accepting and moving past embarrassing, vulnerable moments.

I wasn't fully prepared for what was to come. Rehab was like a school where I learned to live again. My experience with rehab to that point had been limited to the short period of time after my skin grafts and one week working with Rehab Without Walls while at home.

I hadn't gotten over my morning humiliation when my occupational therapist (OT) burst into the room with the exuberance of a cheerleader. "I've got your breakfast. I'm going to teach you how to eat today. I hope you like yogurt."

My "Uh, okay," wasn't exactly a confident start to the first

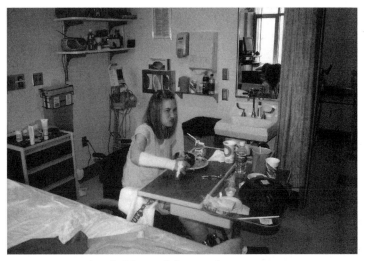

At the rehab hospital, learning how to eat again.

challenge of the day, but if she expected me to do it, I figured there must be a way. A spoon was strapped to my hand, and I waved it in the general area of the bowl. The OT watched intently, evaluating all my movements.

I failed several times before she took my hand and tapped the bowl with the spoon. "Listen to the sound. If you tap the area around the bowl, you can tell its general size, depth, and circumference."

I tapped at the yogurt and missed. With more tapping, I managed to knock the bowl over and poke myself with the spoon. Once I did get it loaded with yogurt, it ended up all over my face, because I couldn't see where the spoon was in relation to my mouth. Food got on my nose, cheek, and chin. I couldn't wipe it off, because there was a spoon strapped to my hand. To top it all off, a stranger sat across the table watching me fail.

Knowing that most two-year-olds can feed themselves, I resisted the urge to pound my hand on the table in frustration. At thirty-three years old, I thought I should have been able to eat. I gained new understanding into why children throw their food.

After my yogurt failure, the therapist cheerfully said, "Let's have you get a drink."

I hesitated. "I don't think I can." I didn't even know where to begin.

"I'd like to watch you try."

Preparing myself, I felt around the table with my right hand. Much of the skin had been damaged by DIC. The resulting nerve damage from the skin grafts left little feeling. I tried to hold the cup with my hand and left residual, but the cup clattered onto the table while water dribbled on the floor. I muttered under my breath.

"Let's have you use a straw for now. I think that would work better." Getting a straw in my mouth was hard but possible. The OT's careful evaluation of my abilities, which had made me so uncomfortable, was what led to my eventual success. All of the therapists I worked with adapted exercises based on my specific disabilities and needs.

They must've known what a disaster breakfast would be, because my next challenge was showering. Being seen in such a vulnerable state stung at my personal sense of modesty. I couldn't see the people looking at me, so I felt like I was being stared at. Wounds and scars covered my body. I imagined I looked like some kind of monstrosity from a horror movie.

Showering was completely different with my disabilities. I sat in a chair while the nurse turned the showerhead away from me and turned on the spray. A shower mitt replaced a washcloth. As I swallowed the shame of showering in front of a stranger, there was a sadness that sunk deeper into my soul. I would never stand in the shower again. It was a small piece of myself that was gone—basic and simple but sorely missed.

After eating and showering, my energy was completely spent, but that was only the beginning. After showering, bandages needed to be replaced, followed by the difficult task of getting dressed. The wound across my back made dressing particularly challenging. It also limited my wardrobe to athletic pants and shirts with no bra—not my usual choice in clothing. Not only did my body feel strange, but the clothes I wore felt alien to me.

Once I was dressed, Mike, my physical therapist (PT), showed up. He began teaching me to use a slide board that would allow me to move from my bed to a wheelchair and from a wheelchair to the shower. It demanded upper body strength and, because I had only one hand, extra coordination. Practicing was awkward and, with my still-recovering grafts, painful.

Next, I was taken to the gym for a more traditional workout. Heath came along to watch as I did sit-ups and rolled from side to side. Strengthening my core and regaining range of motion in my arms was critical to successfully caring for myself. Disuse and trauma had left my coordination similar to that of a toddler. My years of gymnastics, softball, volleyball, and running weren't enough to prevent the deterioration of my body. I had to learn muscle control all over again.

I was so tired at the end of the first morning that I couldn't begin to feed myself. I didn't even want to eat, but Heath insisted. As he fed me as he would a child, I had to remind him not to give me Heath-sized bites. Grateful for a break, I was humbled yet again by how little I could do. With muscles limp and shaky, I hoped for a rest after such an eventful morning.

But inpatient rehab leaves little time for rest. There was too much to do. After lunch, the occupational and physical therapists each came in turn, expecting nothing less than my best effort. I barely kept myself going. Lying in bed that night, I was so exhausted I didn't care that I was alone. The second day was no easier than the first, but I knew what to expect. Hard work and frustration were steps on the path to recovery, and I was to become familiar with them both. While I was learning valuable skills, I was also learning how to trust again.

I was adapting to my new disabilities. My hearing had begun to compensate for my lack of vision. When my family was around, they offered a running monologue of what was happening in the room and made sure I knew who entered. But at rehab, I had to start thinking about doing things for myself, like greeting people. I found I could identify the nurses and therapists by their voices. I didn't know I could do that until I had to. My confidence grew when I could correctly identify which nurse or therapist walked through the door. Calling them by name after they'd said hello was like smiling at them from across the room. Connecting with other people was a piece of myself I'd begun to reclaim.

Those exhausting first two days also brought with them a trickle of hope. I would have to fight to keep that hope as darkness threatened to swallow me all over again.

That Wednesday, my third full day in rehab, Heath walked into my room quieter than usual. His "Hi, Carol," lacked his usual sense of humor. It held a touch of fatigue and heaviness of tone that told me something was wrong.

I waited to see if he would elaborate. When he didn't offer more, I gave him my usual, "Hey."

"How are you this morning?" he asked in the same flat voice. "Did you have a good night?"

The human voice is a strange thing. It communicates with more than words. I sensed a struggle taking place inside my brother. One that he didn't want me to know about but that was so strong he couldn't hide it.

"I'm good. No problems during the night." I waited, but he stayed uncharacteristically silent. "Heath, is something wrong?"

"What makes you ask that?"

"You're my brother. I know you. What's going on?"

Taking a deep, cleansing breath, probably to patch the holes in the secret he was hiding, he continued, "Just . . . it's nothing you need to worry about right now." There it was— a hitch in his voice. Heath is a strong man, not one to be overly emotional, but his speech thickened and he cleared his throat.

"No. Something is wrong. You have to tell me."

"Carol, I don't want you to worry. Okay?"

"Heath, what's going on?"

The legs of a chair scraped across the floor as he sat down hard next to my bed. His fingers rustled through his hair and then pulled down his face as if he were wiping something away. "Not yet. I don't want to be the one to tell you."

The hair on the back of my neck prickled. Something terrible must have happened.

"Please? You have to tell me. It will be okay."

I heard his jacket shift. I imagined his head looking up at me and seeing my blind eyes.

"It's Shawn."

"Shawn?"

"Last night something bad happened. He's in the hospital. I have to drive to eastern Washington today to be with him. Your dad is on his way here right now to be with you."

"Oh, no. What happened?"

"Shawn was drinking with a friend last night. He took something. I'm not sure what. It wasn't a huge amount or anything, but he passed out and his heart stopped beating."

An audible gasp came out as the muscles in my chest constricted in fear.

"His friend didn't do CPR or take him to the hospital for two hours." Heath paused, pushing down anger and digging for the strength to say more. "He's on life support, and they're not sure he's going to make it." He finished with his voice barely above a whisper.

An involuntary "No!" escaped me. My mouth hung open and tears pricked my eyes. The truth sucked the air out of the room. We silently sat together, each of us caught in our own thoughts, waiting for my dad to come. Wrestling with my morning yogurt didn't seem important. Nothing seemed important, only my family.

Heath didn't waste time once my dad arrived. "I'll call you," he said as he walked out the door.

Hours later, after an awful day of waiting, we got the call. I knew in my heart Shawn wasn't going to make it. I'd fought the feeling all day.

Hearing Heath say, "He's brain dead with no possibility of

recovery," made time stop. I didn't know my world could exist without Shawn.

Heath went on, "The doctor said they could keep his body alive but he'll never walk across the room. Mom and I have decided not to prolong this. Shawn wouldn't want to live like that."

Through my tears, I agreed. Even though I knew this was the right decision, I imagined Shawn's hands on the sides of my face as he kissed my forehead goodbye only a few days before. I wasn't there to see my mom stroke his face for the last time as she told him it was okay for him to go. Once life support was stopped, he passed away within a few minutes.

I got off the phone with Heath and fell into my dad's arms. In an empty hospital room, we grieved a loss we had never expected.

The initial overwhelming grief made it hard to breathe or think. I cried until tears wouldn't fall. Nurses came in, but I didn't hear their words. Just when I thought I was finally getting a grip on my life, putting my body back together, my heart shattered with a piece breaking away that would never come back.

I helped my mom pick out a casket and flowers. Heath and I chose music to play in the background, and Heath made a slide show with pictures of Shawn's life.

As much as I wanted to shut out the world, I had to prepare to go to the funeral. Practical considerations were also pressing against me. It was no easy task. I had to get special permission from the hospital so they would hold my spot in rehab. I also had to find a way to travel by car for four hours when I couldn't sit up for long in a moving vehicle. By

Friday morning, I was in a motor home on a road trip with Scott, his sister Brie, Chloe, and Safiya on our way to eastern Washington.

Strapped to a bench across from the dining table, I rolled back and forth the entire trip. I would hit the back of the bench only to then feel the seat belt tug against my stomach as we straightened out again. Driving over Snoqualmie Pass, with its winding turns and hills, the rolling reached a ridiculous level. I pictured myself tumbling like clothes in a dryer. I couldn't hold in the laughter. The ridiculousness of flopping across the seat caused a deep belly laugh to burst out as I continued to roll back and forth.

I yelled to Scott, "What are you doing? Stay on the road!"

Scott and Brie couldn't help but laugh with me.

"That was the first time I knew you were going to be okay," Brie told me months later. "That was a laugh I hadn't heard since before you were sick." Even amidst more tragedy, the old Carol was there, waiting to surface.

The viewing and funeral managed to be both beautiful and heartbreaking.

At the viewing, Scott pushed my wheelchair to the side of the casket while my mom talked softly beside me. "He has on his brown pinstripe suit. He looks so handsome. You can't tell everything he's been through." Shawn had struggled with drugs and alcohol for a few years before his death, taking a hard physical toll.

My hand had to serve as my eyes. I reached out, searching for where to leave my final goodbye. "I just want to touch him," I told my mom. She helped me reach my hand to his chest. The cold stiffness didn't fit with the Shawn I knew. His love and warmth had pulled me through one of the lowest points of my life a short week earlier.

Moving my hand to the fine material of his suit, I pictured his face when we'd snowboarded together. His bright blue eyes lit up in the outdoors. At six feet two inches tall, his broad-shouldered, athletic frame was hard to miss. In my mind, I could hear his laughter at one of his own outrageous jokes told while he wore fake, dollar-store teeth. I found his hand to leave a final squeeze. But, in death, they weren't the hands I remembered.

For Shawn's service, I entered a church for the first time in years. It wasn't just any building. It was the one I had attended for years while growing up. I'd spent hours there with friends at parties, events, and meetings. Though I couldn't see it, the distinct smell of the carpet and echo of footsteps in the gym brought a flood of memories. As a child, walking through the doors of that church had often brought a feeling of comfort and peace. As a grown woman in a wheelchair, those same feelings washed over me when I needed them most.

Hundreds of people showed up for the service. Despite Shawn's troubles, people couldn't help but be drawn to his magnetic personality. His willingness to do anything for a laugh endeared him to many, yet his sensitive soul was as at home writing poetry as it was doing backflips to show off.

Friends from my childhood participated in the service, expressing their sympathy and grieving alongside us. It was good to know others would miss Shawn. A steady stream of people visited with us after the funeral. I talked with them for so long I didn't get a chance to eat.

The next day was spent with friends and family at my

childhood home. Being there, reminiscing over old photos, offered the solace we all needed. The same high school friends who'd visited me in the hospital came to see me then, too. We laughed about our old antics and cried at the losses we'd suffered since our youth. One of them, Erica, drove back with us the following day. She came to stay with me at the hospital for a week.

I threw myself into rehab when I returned. A new set of questions ran through my thoughts. During the day, I focused on therapy, but at night I lay awake wondering why. *Why Shawn? Why me?* No one had answers, least of all me.

All the questions floating through my every waking moment led me to pray for the first time in years. I hoped that if I acted in faith, I might gain understanding. I didn't know what I believed in, but I remembered the comfort I'd experienced as a child attending church. I wanted and needed more of that comfort. Prayer seemed like the right place to begin.

To some questions there will never be answers, but almost immediately I noticed that small comforts came when I needed them.

"Good morning," the morning nurse said as she entered the room, her words tinged with a slight accent from the Philippines.

"Good morning," I said, but there was no feeling behind the words. My heart ached, and my body and spirit were exhausted.

This nurse was a sweet person whom I would come to love and trust. "There is a butterfly on your ceiling this morning. Did you know?"

"No." I wondered if butterfly wings made a sound. "Is it pretty?"

"It's beautiful, with small blue wings. In my country, we believe when a butterfly enters your house, it means your loved ones are watching over you."

Her belief in the power of a tiny butterfly profoundly impacted me. She believed in something greater than herself as a source of comfort. I wondered if I could do the same. I chose to see the butterfly as the first small answer to my prayer.

Comfort and peace continued to come in small, butterfly-like doses and let me set grief aside enough to focus on the challenges at hand. Having Erica at the hospital provided the company I needed when it was easy to feel alone in my suffering. Grief lingered underneath while I threw myself whole-heartedly into the rehab process. The rigorous schedule continued, leaving my muscles shaking at the end of each day.

Shawn's death gave me the ability to see my life as a gift that I didn't want to waste. I'd turned to the faith of my youth in the hope of understanding my current situation. I often asked myself the question, *What would Shawn want me to do?* Giving up, going home, and withering away was not what he would have wanted for me. Rehab was the best way to make something of the life I'd been given.

Shawn's passing gave me another gift: purpose. My mom continued her regular visits, but the nature of those visits changed. She had always been a source of comfort, talking me through nightmares or anxiety attacks. After Shawn's death, she often sat next to my bed in silence. The quiet spoke volumes of the hurt she suffered inside.

"Mom, come lie next to me," I'd say. Without protest, she'd

lie down where I could put my arms around her and hold her as she'd held me so many times before. We grieved together.

"We'll get through this," I would whisper.

I listened to Heath's anger, frustration, and hurt at Shawn's loss as well. Like my mom, I offered reassurance and an understanding heart. It was the first time since my illness that I was needed. They needed me. To be needed added purpose to my existence and tenacity to my rehab sessions.

Even as physical recovery progressed, the mental and emotional implications of my disabilities and Shawn's death threatened to disable me in other ways. I couldn't process all the emotions I experienced on my own. Shelly, a psychotherapist who had worked with me during the grafting process, started visiting me at rehab. She technically wasn't supposed to come, but we connected with one another so well that she got permission from the hospital to help me.

She used hypnotherapy, a practice that involves guided relaxation, concentration, and focused attention to treat any number of mental and physical ailments. Guided relaxation helped me deal with anxiety and depression, two conditions common amongst trauma victims. She made hypnotherapy CDs using her own voice.

Erica and I listened to Shelly's CD mentally guide me to the beach, where I felt the grit of the sand and smelled the salty air. Closing my eyes, I heard the sound of waves. Their rhythmic washing upon the shore pulled the tension from my body as I escaped from the hospital for a short time.

"What do you think of the CD?" I asked Erica.

Her voice held doubt. "I think these CDs are meant only for you."

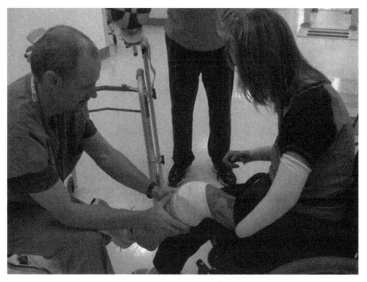

Putting on a pair of prosthetic legs.

We laughed. Those CDs let me escape into my own mind. For brief moments, I could forget my physical and emotional struggles.

Within a few days of my return to the rehab hospital, my first pair of prosthetic legs was ready. Even when I was sitting in a chair, they felt like heavy weights hanging from my legs. I couldn't simply strap them on and start walking. Mike, my physical therapist, showed Heath how to attach them. He knew it would be a while before I could do it myself. All the while, Mike talked about sockets, suspension sleeves, and other terminology I didn't know applied to a leg. It sounded like a foreign language. There was so much I had yet to learn.

My dad, Judy, Heath, and Erica watched from the side as I was strapped to a tilt table that slowly inclined, letting me feel the weight of the prosthetics tugging at my legs. When I finally

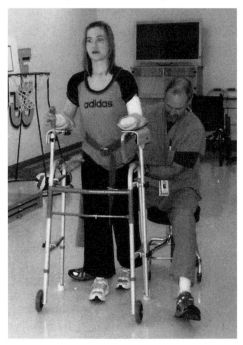

Standing on prosthetic legs and learning to walk.

stood, I gripped my walker with all my strength. It was like standing on two-by-fours.

"Easy," Mike said, steadying me. "I want you to stay put for a minute. Feel out your new legs. I have to grab something. I'll be right back."

"Okay," I muttered. Standing was tough work that took all my concentration. After lying and sitting for so many weeks, I felt like a towering giant. The faces of my family, most clearly my girls, flashed through my mind. How could I just stand there and wait when Chloe and Safiya needed me at home?

Ignoring Mike's instructions, I picked up one heavy foot and jerked it forward. Gaining confidence, I shifted my

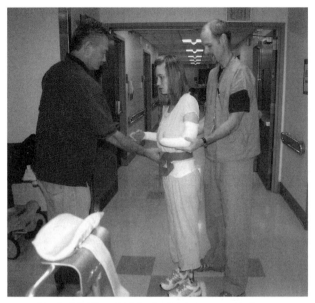

My dad (left) and Mike (right) helping with therapy.

weight and picked up the other one, clunking it down with Frankenstein-like grace.

Mike's smiling voice held surprise and something I liked: admiration. "Well, so that's how it's going to be."

"Yup," I said with glee. Two steps toward my girls.

From then on, I fully surrendered myself to the rehab process. Instead of succumbing to the grief of Shawn's death, I pushed for something better: my family.

Mike and the other therapists asked me to do things I didn't think I could. Whether it was getting down on my knees, walking 400 feet, or moving pegs on a pegboard, I trusted them. My favorite answer became, "If you think I can do it, I'll try."

Slow, steady progress came through trust and a willing

attitude. My willingness to try had an effect on my progress that was obvious to Scott when I came home on the weekends. His surprise when I could roll over or slide from the bed to my wheelchair drove me to try even harder.

My first weekend home was spent going to dinner and a Sigur Rós concert in downtown Seattle with my mom, Heath, Scott, and a friend of Shawn's who had been unable to come to the funeral. We went to my favorite restaurant, Wild Ginger. As I rode in my wheelchair, the tangy scents and tastes were a decadent pleasure. Scott cut up all my food and brought along a special fork with a thick handle for me to use. I was able to get a few bites myself, but, in the end, Scott fed me. The concert was the same music Heath had played in the background at Shawn's funeral. The beauty and memories it evoked penetrated deep, causing tears to pour down my cheeks.

Spending a weekend with my family fueled my determination for the next week of grueling therapy. I knew there were possibilities awaiting me, and I was going to reach them.

Mike watched me successfully use a slide board. "You're doing great. Using a slide board is another check on the list."

The word *list* caught my attention. "What list?"

"We have a list of milestones for you to meet before you can go home. Using the slide board is another one down."

"Will you read me the list?" I listened, paying close attention. I loved goals and still do. A willingness to try and a step-by-step plan to follow was the combination I needed to accelerate my recovery. I had weekly meetings with my doctor, therapists, nurses, Scott, and Heath in which we talked about my progression down the list. Each week I got closer and closer to being back with my family. But, even as I worked toward completing the list, I dealt with disappointment and discouragement.

Erin brought the girls to see me every week. At first, the visits didn't go as I'd hoped.

"Hi, Carol," Erin called as she pushed the door open.

"Hi!" My heart raced, anticipating Chloe running to tell me about her day. I heard the closet door open, quickly followed by Erin's, "Chloe, come out of there. Come say hi to Mommy."

Her feet landed hard on the linoleum. "No."

"Chloe." I pretended her childish "no" didn't hurt. "Did you bring bunny?"

"No." She'd already moved to my nightstand, pulling open the drawers.

"Go say hi to Mom." Erin's voice strained as she picked Chloe up and brought her closer to me.

"No."

The hospital was a scary place with strange people and sounds. Chloe was more interested in crawling on the floor and opening all the drawers than she was in me. My appearance scared her, and we only saw each other briefly on weekends. Hearing my daughter's fear caused a wound deeper than any on my body.

"It's okay, Erin," I lied.

"I'll lay Safiya on the bed next to you." She placed a reassuring hand on my shoulder.

"Do you want to feed Safiya using your new brace?" One of my OT therapists had made a brace for my hand that allowed me to hold a baby bottle.

"Yeah, let's do it." Erin helped me get the brace on and snapped the bottle in place.

"Can you help me get it to her mouth? I'm worried I'm going to poke her in the eye."

Erin guided my hand to Safiya. Hearing her sucking and swallowing fulfilled my need to do *something* for my baby.

"What are these, Mommy?" Chloe called from the end of my bed.

"What does she have, Erin?" I turned my head to Chloe, trying to determine what she was looking at.

"Your prosthetics."

"Chloe, those are Mommy's new feet. What do you think?" Chloe's curiosity was insatiable.

"They don't look like my feet."

I laughed, pleased that she would talk to me even though she wouldn't come near me. "No, they don't."

Engaging Chloe was a constant struggle. I finally asked Erin, "How do I get her to come near me?"

"Do you have any treats or anything you can give her when we visit?"

I thought for a moment. Sugary treats were not on the menu that often. But then I remembered. "I can order Froot Loops with my breakfast. I'll save some for the next time you come."

Bribery worked. Chloe started running to me as soon as she came in my hospital room. I knew she was excited for the cereal, but it was a small step toward acceptance.

When they left, I missed Chloe's tiny voice bouncing off the walls and her feet pattering on the floor.

I'd ask the nurses, "Did you see my babies? Aren't they

beautiful?" I couldn't stop talking about them. More than anything, I wanted to be their mother. I wanted to run after them, sweep Chloe into my arms, and hold her while we laughed together. I pictured myself rocking and singing to Safiya. A sharp pain filled my heart at all I'd lost.

Surrendering to rehab meant pushing doubts aside, replacing them with the hope that rehab would get me to the point where I could be a mother again. Trusting my therapists let me start to regain some independence.

As I sat at home one weekend, I exercised my independence to get closer to Chloe. I sat listening to her talk to her toys, break out into periodic songs, and work her way around the room. From my wheelchair, I tracked her movements.

"Fish," she said as clearly as a two-year-old could. She stood directly in front of me. "Come watch the fish."

"Are you going to watch the fish on your TV?" I asked. The last movie we'd seen together before my illness was *Finding Nemo*. Chloe had a toy TV with fish that swam across the picture.

She tugged on my hand, trying to pull me forward with her. Thrilled that she was willing to touch me, I tried to figure out how I could do what she wanted. "Fish. Mommy come see the fish."

"Oh, well, I'm not sure . . ."

"Please. Come see the fish with me."

I hesitated, but not for long. I would do anything for her. "Okay, give Mommy a minute." I turned myself in the wheelchair and slid my knees to the ground.

"Come. Come see the fish!" Chloe yelled again from a few feet away.

I crawled across the floor using my elbows and knees until I was close enough to feel her squirming body against mine.

"See the fish, Mommy?"

"Uh, yes." I said, happy to be lying next to her. "What color are they?"

"There's a blue one and look, look, there's a yellow one."

"Is there a Nemo fish?"

"Oh, yes. He's orange and white."

A brilliant idea struck me. "Does he have a lucky fin?"

"Yes. I see his lucky fin. It's too small."

"Can you see my arm?" I held out my left residual. "Mommy has a lucky fin too. Just like Nemo."

She squealed and clapped happily. "You have a lucky fin!"

Chloe talked about the fish for a while longer before moving on to another toy. I didn't know how I would get back into my chair, but I didn't care. It was the first time Chloe had interacted with me much at all. I was in utter bliss and would have lain there all day if she'd wanted. We still call my left arm my lucky fin.

For that short moment, I was her mother again. That wonderful "mommy" feeling is what I wanted. It was a taste of what I hoped my life could be once I made it through rehab. Each weekend I spent at home fueled me toward reaching that goal.

At rehab, I talked about my beautiful girls. My therapists used my girls as a motivator. They developed exercises that would help me reconnect with Chloe and Safiya. I worked the hardest on skills that would help me take care of my children. Working on wooden puzzles and diapering a baby doll were some of the tasks my therapists hoped would come in handy later on. The more fully I gave in to the rehab process, the closer I moved toward my goal of becoming a mother again.

Rehab also opened doors to connecting with other people like me—people whose lives had been shattered. In the room next door was a man paralyzed from the waist down in a diving accident. As I slowly walked past his room on my prosthetics, he would say, "I wish I had legs like yours, so I could walk."

I always replied, "I wish I had eyes like yours, so I could see where I'm going." Our shared experience of loss brought us together despite our differences in disabilities.

It took five weeks to check everything off the list. Intensive inpatient therapy gave me the jump start I needed. During that time, I built relationships with therapists, doctors, nurses, and other patients. I used my prosthetics for a couple hours a day and continued to work on feeding and other daily tasks. I could brush my teeth, as long as someone handed me the toothbrush. I could get dressed, as long as someone gave me the clothes right side out and facing the correct direction. I could use a slide board, as long as someone placed it for me first. But I still had a long way to go. I couldn't put on my prosthetics myself, stand by myself, or push my wheelchair. The small measures of independence I had accomplished were the light I needed to see through the darkness.

Coming out of the darkness gave me the ability to clearly see that the shattered pieces of my life weren't all unfixable. I had already begun to reclaim some, but others still seemed far out of reach. More struggles were ahead, but even a tiny spark of hope kept the darkness at bay.

CHAPTER 8

—— ❧ ——

Exist or Live

"Everything can be taken from a man but one thing: the last of the human freedoms—to choose one's attitude in any given set of circumstances, to choose one's own way."
—*Viktor E. Frankl*

Shaky and unsteady, I stepped out of the waters of sepsis onto a shore of possibilities. I'd won the battle between physical life and death. Yet, I couldn't walk on my own, feed myself an entire meal, push my wheelchair, or get showered by myself. I could perform singular steps within multistep processes. Coming home overwhelmed me with the reality of living with my disabilities. Confidence that was so hard won in rehab seemed to slip away. Looking ahead, I could see only two paths before me.

One path was straight and devoid of obstacles but ugly and barren. I could let other people take and maintain control over my daily decisions while I watched from the sidelines. On this path, I would wait at home for people to come to me. I wouldn't pursue my own interests or become involved in the world outside. Progress, goals, and fulfillment would be absent as my body and mind atrophied. The goal would be existence and nothing more.

But there was another path. It would be difficult, and I didn't know the final destination. Obstacles were scattered along the way that changed the path's course. There were no guarantees of success, but at the end I would do more than exist. I would *live*. There were possibilities for happiness and joy, heartache and triumph, all created by a willingness to try.

I had to make a choice—exist or live.

For months I didn't live; I existed. Doctors, nurses, and my family did what was necessary to keep me alive. For a time, that was enough because I was a victim. Sepsis acted on my body without my consent. All my family and I could do was ride out the waves until it passed.

I made the first, diminutive step out of darkness when I chose not to take my own life. At the very least, I chose existence. Yet I remained directionless and afraid. Rehab gave me the tools I needed to continue moving toward recovery. I learned I could improve. I clung to the hope that if I kept trying, I would eventually be able to brush my own teeth from start to finish or transfer from my wheelchair to the sofa or get dressed on my own. If I could care for myself, maybe, eventually, I could take care of Chloe and Safiya as well. I forced myself to believe that if I kept going, happiness would drown pain and loss.

I knew I wanted to live, to experience life alongside Scott, Chloe, and Safiya. I didn't know if that desire was possible, nor did I know how to accomplish it. Bandages, which would remain for another year, still covered my legs, arm, hand, and back. Changing, cleaning, and dressing my wounds took two hours every morning. Family members came each day to help watch the girls or get me ready. Though I lived in the same house with my husband and children, by necessity, my days were spent recovering and rehabilitating. In the meantime, the girls played and grew. We lived our lives next to each other, with me watching and listening from another room. I didn't know how to become a part of their lives again.

My family and friends had held the pieces of my life together while sepsis attacked my body. They were ready and willing to give me back the pieces as I grew stronger, but I didn't know what to do with them. I didn't know who I was or who I could become. I was afraid the most important piece—being a mother—was gone. That one part of my identity was what kept me from taking my life. If there was even a small possibility that I could be a mother again, life was worth living.

If I was going to live, I had to choose—give up or pick up.

Without the demanding therapy schedule of the hospital, I now had time to think and ponder, time to let my imagination run, and time for questions and doubts to linger. Coming home again put me face to face with all the reasons I had to survive while at the same time revealing how far I had to go. I struggled with the same challenges I'd had the first time I came home. However, this time I was better equipped to deal with them. My family and Erin helped me with everything from placing and moving the slide board to maneuvering my wheelchair around the kitchen table. I was in the process of learning and becoming efficient at self-care, but there was little I did well. Eating was still a mess. I got better at dressing and caring for myself, but I had to ask for help with most basic tasks. All aspects of my day were chaotic and stressful.

The basic building blocks were there—family, love, support—to make my life work. But I didn't know how to use them to become a wife, mother, and confident woman. Not only that; I realized the path was longer than I had imagined. I was looking at years of in-home rehab.

Weeks after coming home, I was still discouraged. "I still can't change Safiya's diaper," I told Scott. "They keep trying to teach me to use the hook on the prosthetic, but it doesn't work for me. I'm going to poke someone's eye out. I can't get Chloe's tights on with one hand. I can't get my legs on myself. How will I take care of the girls?" I feared the girls would never see me as their mother.

"Right now, you need to focus on getting better."

Listening to his voice calmed me. We sat on the couch, the girls already in bed. With family, friends, and therapists in and out of the house all day, every day, quiet time alone was rare.

"Do you think our lives are always going to be like this?" I wondered aloud.

"Which part do you mean?"

"Will we ever live alone with our children in our own house? Will I be able to help them get ready for school and go to their activities?" My voice caught in my throat. "I don't know if I'll ever be able to take care of the girls."

Scott let out a heavy sigh. "Give it time." The heaviness of the burden he carried added audible weight to his voice. "I know it doesn't always feel like it, but you've made so much progress. You're getting better every day."

"I want to be their mother. Not just another person in the

room." At that point, I couldn't pick Chloe up to put her on my lap. If I couldn't *act* like their mom, how would they know I was their mom? I expressed my fear the best I could, though saying it aloud nearly killed me. "I'm afraid the girls are going to miss out because of my disabilities. I want them to experience a normal childhood."

"As long as we are together on this, I think we can give them all the things we had growing up and more." Scott reached over and brushed my hair behind my ear before stroking my cheek. "I want to give them a life full of the same opportunities we had, and so do you. If that's our goal, we can make it happen."

"I just don't want them to. . . ." Emotion choked my words. I was so tired of crying, but the tears inevitably fell several times a week.

"We'll figure it out." Scott kissed me. "Let's get you ready for bed before you fall asleep."

He brought out the compression socks that had replaced leg immobilizers. As Scott strapped on my hand brace, I appreciated all he did for me. I never thought he would have to care for me like this when we were still so young. We continued talking until I fell asleep. His calm reassurance made it seem as though everything would turn out for the best. I was aware but not fully awake when he carried me to bed.

Those moments between us were so rare that I feared for our marriage almost as much as I feared the girls wouldn't see me as their mother. Scott and I had a difficult truth to face. Trauma is hard on more than the mind and body. The divorce rate for couples that endure trauma like mine is high. Physical, mental, and financial stress can tear a marriage apart. I did not want my marriage to be a victim of sepsis the way my body was.

I couldn't imagine a life without Scott, but we broke out into arguments that would've never happened before my illness. We differed in how we dealt with stress, creating a combustible atmosphere. Even amidst our arguments, I depended on him. He became the nurturer, a role that had always been mine. He took care of me no matter the disagreement. He carried me to the shower and transferred me to my wheelchair. He dressed and adjusted my clothing to fit just right.

He sat inches from my face holding a makeup compact. "What do I do with the powder stuff?"

"You already put foundation on, so you brush it over the top. Lightly. It just makes it so my face doesn't look shiny."

"Yeah, okay." Bristles floated over my face. He grimaced and used his fingers to wipe my cheek. "Too much right there."

I fought a smile so as not to disturb his concentration. I talked him through the whole process, my love and appreciation growing with every stroke. "Thank you," I said, but two words seemed too small to express the true depth of my gratitude.

Relying on hope, we worked to connect and draw strength from one another rather than rip each other apart. Scott's way of dealing with the stress was to find solutions. If he found or even heard of a tool he thought might make my life easier, he bought it. He bought a push-button can opener, talking computer, label-making pen that responded to my voice, and a color reader to tell me the color of my clothing. The list could go on and on. I learned to be careful what I mentioned, because if he thought it would help or make me happy, it would show up on my front doorstep. I knew he loved me and would do anything in his power to help me succeed in my recovery.

In contrast, I needed to talk. For months, I worked through the most difficult emotions with different therapists, but Scott was always an integral part of my recovery. He listened while I talked, and sometimes that was all I needed. I used my wedding ring as a physical reminder of my commitment. I hadn't been able to wear it since my left hand had been taken, so I put the ring on a necklace to keep it close to my heart. It also served as a symbol of where I wanted to be—with a complete family that included me in it.

Scott's unwavering confidence strengthened me when I faltered.

He would often tell me, "You are going to be so amazing that people are going to want to be like you."

When he told me that, I couldn't help but scoff. "No, they won't. That's ridiculous. Why would they want to be like me?"

"You're a great mom. You'll be so good on your prosthetics people will want legs like yours." I may not have believed him, but there was power in his confidence.

My emotions swung like a pendulum. I'd wake in the morning with optimism only to be frustrated the next day by my perceived shortcomings. I often turned to Erin as a confidant. As my daily companion, she was there for the most vulnerable parts of my day.

"How many blind triple amputees do you know?" I asked without warning.

"You're the only one." Erin answered with the gentle patience that is part of her nature.

"Exactly. No one will want to be friends with me."

"Just be yourself." The familiar touch of her hand on my shoulder released the growing tension deep inside. "Talk to people. If you put yourself out there, you'll find more friends than you think." I trusted Erin's counsel, even though I didn't believe her at the time.

Putting my faith in Erin and the therapists who regularly worked with me was natural. I'd connected with people at rehab, but they were either staff or other people recovering from traumatic injuries like me. Connecting with people outside of my immediate family and the small group of professionals I worked with seemed like an impossible task.

People often came to our house bringing gifts, flowers, and well wishes. Members of the community and our congregation brought dinner over several times a week for months. They frequently asked how I was doing and wanted to say hello. I was grateful for their kindness, but I didn't want to talk to them. More accurately, I didn't want them to see me. Not being able to see myself, I could only imagine what I must have looked like in their eyes.

I didn't feel like I belonged and I wanted to be left alone.

After yet another person brought dinner, asked how I was doing, and faced my one-word reply, Erin's usually quiet footsteps carried extra force. When she'd tried to hide a sigh, I finally asked, "Is something wrong?"

Ever diplomatic and sensitive, she said, "Can I tell you how I see it?"

"Of course." I waited, not sure I really wanted to hear what she had to say.

"You're worried about how people look at you. That's only

Receiving encouragement at the Enumclaw fund-raiser.

natural. But you forget that they want to help you. They'd like to be friends."

"I appreciate what they're doing," I replied, "but how am I supposed to make friends? What am I going to say? No one *is* like me. How will we relate to one another?"

"You are unique. But they want to help and bless you. They are offering a part of themselves. When you accept their service, their charity, you're allowing blessings to come into their lives, too. Don't worry so much about what to say. Be yourself. You'll be surprised how much you might have in common."

I'd spent years working in the medical field putting patients at ease before I drew blood or performed some other procedure. Talking and connecting with people was a piece of my personality that had always been there. I had to put it to use in my new situation. So I did. I opened up and talked to people. I let them see me.

As it turned out, everyone who came to the house had a story. When I put myself out there and listened, I learned that everyone had experienced loss of some kind. I found support and understanding from people who'd been trying to give it all along. Friends offered their help and often a shoulder to cry on.

One afternoon, Erin came into my room saying, "Lori's here. She wants to know if she can take Chloe with her to the park. Is that okay?"

Lori and I had been friends for only a year when I got sick. Our friendship had developed easily, as she and I were both talkers and never ran out of things to say. She was a regular visitor while I was in the hospital and had run a marathon to raise money for my medical expenses. "Oh, of course," I said, but I was surprised by a spark of jealousy.

"She'd like to come back and say hi," Erin said.

Lori was a good friend, and I knew I should say something to her, but she was doing something I never could. She would push Chloe on the swings and see her go down the slide, and I wouldn't. In that moment, she represented all that I couldn't be, all that I couldn't do.

Still, I swallowed my feelings and told Erin to bring her to my room.

"Hi, Carol. I'm excited to take Chloe with us." Lori's cheerful nature flowed through her words. "Have you already done therapy today?"

I lay on the bed without prosthetics or braces. It was me, alone and raw. "Yes, therapy went well today. I told the therapist that I'm going to walk in high heels someday. I don't think she believed me."

"She must not know you very well, then. You're okay with me taking Chloe with us to the park?"

I tried to answer, but my resolve and voice wavered. I couldn't contain my emotions, so I turned my head the other way.

Lori moved closer. Sitting on the bed, she reached out and touched my arm. "Are you okay?"

As much as I wanted to be strong and keep my sadness to myself, I didn't hide it very well. "No," I whispered. My voice cracked. "I can't see them, Lori. I can't watch the girls go down the slide or climb to the top of the jungle gym." I couldn't hold back tears. "*We* should be taking our girls to the park together. I can't see my babies."

"I'm so sorry." Lori put her hand on mine and sat with me. I could hear her fighting her own tears. "You're going to see someday. I know you'll be taking care of the girls sooner than you think. You are a strong person, and you're going to get through this. We all love you and are praying for you." Lori may not have known what it felt like to lose her sight, but she understood grief and loss because it comes to everyone's life at one point or another. She'd lost her father under difficult circumstances only the year before. Though our suffering was different, she sympathized and offered support by giving service and hope. Accepting help was part of accepting myself. But even in my loss, I found motivation.

I realized I wasn't destined to be alone in my disabilities, grief, or recovery as long as I was willing to let others in. With each person I connected to, I moved closer to becoming whole again. Friends, family, and, most importantly, my children gave me the motivation to be a survivor—to live rather than just exist.

If I wanted to take Chloe to the park with Lori, I needed to get up and go. Crying in my room was a natural part of recovery, but I couldn't stay there if I wanted to be the mother I envisioned. Motivation came with a sense of urgency that propelled me forward. I knew the biggest gains in my recovery would come in the first year or two.

I had to stop being a victim and become a survivor. Rehab showed me I could handle the challenges of trauma. But there was another obstacle that was almost as challenging still standing in my way—fear.

I was no stranger to fear. Shawn and Heath taught me fearlessness as I had tried to keep up with them as a child. I remember, as a seven-year-old, looking at a bike jump they'd made from cinder blocks and particleboard.

One of their friends turned to Shawn and said, "She won't do it. She's just a little girl."

My childish pride wouldn't be squashed. I stared at the jump from the banana seat of my yellow bike. I searched for the courage to push the pedals. The jump grew in size the longer I stared at it.

"Yeah, she will. Won't you?" called Shawn through his hands cupped around his mouth.

Heath chimed in, "She's no chicken."

"No way," the doubter said.

I looked him straight in the eye before I glanced at Shawn and Heath.

I pedaled with all my strength toward the jump. With the

tassels on the handles swinging parallel to the ground, I ignored their laughs and calls. My aim wasn't as true as it should have been. I hit far right of center, catapulting the bike and me into a heap on the ground. My face hit the dirt first, followed by my hands and knees.

I heard their "Ooooohh" and the scuffle of feet as they came to stare at me.

I stood up with blood trickling down my hands and knees. "Are you okay?" Heath asked.

With my striped tube socks falling down to my ankles, I shrugged my shoulders. "Yeah, sure." Biting the inside of my cheek, I hoped they didn't look too closely at my watery eyes.

"Geez," the most vocal of the doubters said. "Your little sister is tough. Mine would have bawled like a baby."

"Told you." Shawn punched the kid in the arm before they turned away and disappeared around the corner of the house next door.

Only after I was sure they were gone did I pick up my bike and let the tears fall. My fearlessness and determination were pieces of myself that survived sepsis. I had to dig deep to find them, but when I did, I moved closer to becoming the person I wanted to be.

I had to focus on the job at hand—therapy and recovery. I had in-home therapy three days a week. Before each session started, Erin or Heath attached my prosthetics for me. Walking was slow and awkward. I wore a three-inch gait belt around my waist, giving my therapist something to hold while we worked. It became my least favorite accessory during rehab sessions.

Sitting in my wheelchair, preparing myself to stand, the

therapist held the belt at the small of my back. "Okay, feel with your feet. Test them out before you use your full weight."

I shifted my feet, paying close attention to where I felt pressure on my legs. I scooted as close to the edge of the chair as I dared. Testing my feet placement, I leaned forward to a shaky crouch, where I put a good portion of my weight on the walker in front of me. My therapist pulled on the belt, giving the added balance I needed to get to my feet.

"Tighten your abs and squeeze your butt. Hold there and widen your stance."

Heavy concentration left no room for an answer. I shuffled my feet until I felt secure. "Okay," I said.

"I'm going to have you do sit-stands. I want you to sit back down, but just before you sit, I want you to stand again."

I took a deep breath and leaned back. The therapist held tight to the belt in case I started falling to one side or the other. I almost reached sitting when she loudly exclaimed, "Now stand."

My arms went out to either side to keep me from falling. I brought my hand forward to the walker and used it to stand again.

After our sessions, my legs ached for hours from the pressure and a progressing problem with a bone spur on the end of the bone in my left leg. But this pain came with progress. The slow changes in my abilities were worth the discomfort. Patience with myself and the process was as important to rehab as the effort I put into it.

In addition to working with Rehab Without Walls, once a week I worked with a family friend named Dan Steel, who was also a physical therapist. He liked to push boundaries and played an important role in my mind-set.

"I want you to hop," he said one session.

"Are you kidding?" I couldn't even wrap my head around the idea. Standing was difficult enough.

"Hop. You know, like a rabbit. I want you to jump." He said it so matter-of-factly, as if he'd forgotten I had metal legs.

"Jump? I can't do that. I'll fall on my face." I chuckled under my breath, but falling posed a real hazard and was something I feared. Jumping was so far above my comfort and skill level I didn't know where to begin.

"I don't want to hear that word."

I thought for a moment. "What word?"

"*Can't.* There is no place for the word *can't.* You're not allowed to use it. You can ask for help, but do not use the word *can't.*" Dan was kind but direct. "I'm next to you, and I'll have my hand on your belt."

"Okay." I still hesitated. "Well, I'll try it, but I don't know."

"You have to get over the fear of what *could* happen and just do it. Once you get over that fear, you're going to be able to do the things you want to do. I won't let you fall. Even if you fail, it doesn't mean you won't succeed next time."

My memory drifted to Chloe. I remembered watching her walk through the grass in our backyard. She came to the edge of the patio, which was only an inch above the grass. Bending down, she placed her chubby hands on the cement and carefully lifted each foot onto the patio before she stood and continued walking to me. I wanted to metaphorically put my hands on the cement and carefully step forward. However, sometimes you have to take a chance.

Dan and my other therapists pushed me past what I thought were my limits. I wanted to go slowly and carefully as Chloe had done, but he knew I could do more. He believed in me when I didn't.

Unsure of how far off the ground I would rise, or how I would land, I braced myself. I focused, trying to figure out how to jump without ankles. Finding my balance and bending my knees, I put my arms out in anticipation. Finally, I pushed off into the air. I barely left the ground, and I landed with a sharp jolt to my legs, but I did it.

I jumped.

Adrenaline heightened the joy that coursed through my body. I'd accomplished something impossible. I'd pushed past what I'd thought were my physical limits. My body was capable of far more than I knew. It was a huge mental step toward being a survivor. As a survivor, I could defeat my own mental odds.

Hard work created opportunities for good things to not only reenter my life but helped me to recognize those moments for the precious gems they were. When I found them, I held them close to my heart to help me cross over obstacles.

Joy came in those small moments.

One Saturday morning I woke early and listened to Scott's gentle breathing. Saturdays were the one morning no one arrived until later in the day. I couldn't see the clock or sun, so I had no reference for time. Instead, I waited for Scott to wake. I imagined his chest rising and falling without the stress that filled both of our days. A rustle of sheets and a soft moan let me know when he'd opened his eyes and turned in my direction.

"Good morning," he said. The bed depressed, rocking me toward him. I leaned my head closer as he placed a kiss on my lips. "Did you sleep okay?"

"Yes, you?"

Before he could answer, a cry sounded over the baby monitor.

"Do you think if I ignore her she'll go back to sleep?" Scott asked lightly.

"That's wishful thinking." I glowed inside at the normalcy of the conversation. It's what we would have done before our lives turned upside down.

He covered the short distance to Safiya's room before her cry got loud enough to wake Chloe. While he prepared a bottle in the kitchen, the familiar sounds of running water and clinking bottles made their way to our room. I couldn't make out his words, but periodically he stopped mid-sentence to give Safiya a kiss. The touch of his lips against her skin traveled in the morning quiet.

His soft whispers accompanied them as they made their way to our bedroom. "I'm going to lay her on the bed while I get a burp rag."

Safiya's grunts and smacking lips were so close I didn't want to move. I tried to sense where she was. "How close to me is she? I don't want to squish her."

"Unless you start rolling around, she's safe," Scott called from the bathroom.

Using my good hand, I slowly felt along the top of the bedspread, searching for her. I tried to hold still, afraid I'd inadvertently bump her off the bed. Scott came back, scooping her up for her morning feeding. I leaned in, wanting to be a part of them.

As Safiya finished her bottle, the *slap, slap, slap* of tiny feet echoed down the hall.

Chloe's chipper, happy voice cut through the stillness with laser sharpness. "Hi!"

"Good morning, muffin," I called. "Do you want to come up on the bed with us and watch cartoons?"

"Yup." Chloe toddled over to Scott's side of the bed. He managed to hold Safiya and hoist Chloe into the bed with ease. I envied him. The bed bounced as her wiggly body joined us.

"Is there enough room? Am I too close to the edge?" I asked, hoping Safiya wouldn't get jostled by Chloe. I worried for their safety even in our king-size bed. My spatial awareness wasn't as highly developed as my hearing. I worried about falling off the bed myself.

"No, you're fine. Chloe, let's find you a cartoon."

Chloe giggled and bounced. Scott muttered something about too many remotes before he found something on TV that caused Chloe to start clapping. "This one!" she exclaimed. She calmed as much as her morning energy allowed. I closed my eyes, taking in the sounds around me.

Lying there, I knew this was something a normal family would experience. We could be normal. Being together doing something we would have done before sepsis was living the life I had imagined.

That was why and how I wanted to live, as a part of their lives, not as a passive observer. I hadn't waited eight years to start a family to let them live their lives without me. They— Scott, Chloe, and Safiya—gave me purpose and a reason to not remain a victim. My days were full of hard work and frustration. I used the happy times, like our Saturday morning together, to see me through when I felt overwhelmed. There were days I kept my head above water by focusing on the positive changes in my situation.

The most difficult setback I faced came a few months after I'd been home. The bone had started breaking through the skin in my left arm. I knew it would mean drugs, needles, and more rehab. Recovery always felt like three steps forward and two steps back.

The discomfort caused by the bone spur, which looked like a fishhook on the end of my bone, had reached a point that it couldn't be ignored any longer. The last step was scheduling the surgery. Heath and I met with Dr. Friedly and Dr. Smith, a world-renowned orthopedic surgeon who had worked in the military.

"I think we can do your arm and leg at the same time. That way you won't have to go through more than one surgery," Dr. Friedly told me.

"We'll revise your left arm, cutting back some of the nerve so you don't have as much pain there," Dr. Smith added.

"Wait," I said. "I don't want too much nerve taken. I have more feeling and sensation with my left arm than my right hand. That's how I see things."

Dr. Smith's military background did not temper his natural kindness. I could hear the smile in his voice as he said, "We'll have to take some. I'll make sure we leave as much as possible, okay?"

"We'll use Dr. Smith's technique on your leg, fusing the bones and creating a bone bridge using the bone spur. That's going to make your leg more stable. We'll take some nerves from there, too, so you don't feel as much pain when you're walking," said Dr. Friedly. Amputations are a complicated business.

Then Dr. Smith dropped news that brought everything crumbling down around me. "We're going to do enough work that you'll need to do inpatient rehab for a time."

My jaw dropped and tears fell before I could fully process. "No. Please, no. I don't want to go back. Please." Weeks away from my family, therapy all day, the loneliness and fear of the unknown—it was more than I could handle. "I can't do that again."

Heath put his arm around me. I buried my head in his shoulder and shamelessly cried.

"Wait, Dr. Smith, Carol does well with therapy at home," Dr. Friedly interjected. She had worked with me for far longer than Dr. Smith. "She thrives there and has a good support system. I think she can do her hospital stay and then complete rehab at home."

"Of course, if you think that will work, we can do that," Dr. Smith agreed.

For two weeks I dreaded the surgery. But even then, the light of hope stayed in my life. Two representatives from our congregation arranged for the children from our church to come to my house after their Sunday meetings and sing for me. On a cloudy Sunday afternoon, I listened to their pure voices sing of faith, hope, and love. My niece was amongst them and sat next to me while a violin accompanied the last song. Although fear troubled me, I couldn't help but feel peace and calm at not only their talents and the time they took to

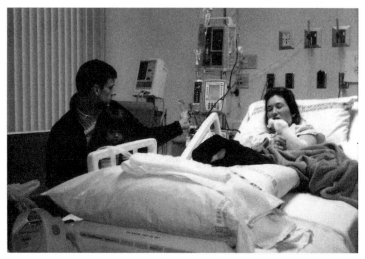

Back to the hospital for more leg surgery.

come but also in the message they shared. *I wasn't alone in my struggles. I never had been.*

When the time came to go to the hospital with Scott and Heath, I became inconsolable. This surgery wasn't as serious as many I'd endured, but the trauma I'd already experienced made it hard to go back to the hospital. I pictured myself being thrown back into deep water, starting my journey over again.

Through tears, I asked, "What if I don't make it?"

"You've made it through more than this," Scott answered. He sat with me while I waited to get prepped for surgery.

"I can't do this." Severe tremors plagued me after surgeries. Mentally, I was back in the days of grafting—depression, anxiety, loneliness.

"You can." Heath took my hand. "We'll be here when you wake up."

And Scott, Heath, my mom, and my dad were there, with

the same support and guidance they'd always offered. I lost sight of my choice for a while, but when I woke I realized I didn't have as far to go as I'd feared.

The choice to live was one I had to fight for because recovery came with setbacks, like more surgeries. Falling back into my old mindset was all too easy. I had to choose to live day after day. But knowing that I'd made that choice gave me resolve and courage. There was nothing left to do but go for it.

Every surgery, every frustration, and every bad day forced me to fight, to rise up again. Sometimes I had to accept or ask for help, but I could do it. The journey was about more than gathering the pieces of my life. I had to rearrange them to fit into my new existence. Time and patience led to a slow, steady progress that moved me toward a destination I had yet to imagine.

CHAPTER 9

Letting Go

"We must be willing to let go of the life we planned
so as to have the life that is waiting for us."
—Joseph Campbell

My physical losses shattered my self-perception, my core identity. My mind was constantly full of questions: *Who am I? Who can I be with my body like this? What will my life be like?* I felt as though I stood atop a mountain looking over a precipice. Was I brave enough to step off into the unknown? But a memory stirred. I had literally stood on top of a mountain before.

• • •

A cold, piercing wind blows over the crest of the mountain against my twelve-year-old face as my brothers and I ride the chairlift to the top of the ski slope. From the bottom, the run didn't look too steep, but as we climb higher I grip the rail of the lift and sink further into the seat. Exhilaration and excitement mingle with fear, enough that I can feel the blood pulsing through my veins. Looking at the board strapped to my foot, a warm glow pushes back. My brothers want me, their little sister, to be with them on the mountain.

The crisp air chills my lungs, making me feel so alive that a giddy smile intermittently flits across my face. Coming to the top of the chairlift, I realize I don't know how to get off. The snowboarders ahead of me slide off with an awkward yet coordinated swaying step. I look to Shawn and Heath, waiting for their words of advice. They say something about a "stomp pad" and "ride it like a skateboard." Despite my best efforts, I stumble off the lift, falling into an uncoordinated heap.

Somehow I drag myself and the board off to the side. My brothers meet me there, ready to teach me the ways of the mountain. With my arms out for balance, I am prepared to learn.

"You ready, Carol?" Heath asks.

"I think so," I say.

"You can do it, just go for it."

Those are the only words of wisdom he offers before he glides away with Shawn. Neither of them gives me a second glance as their boards move away, smooth and serpentine. They've left me sitting at the top of a mountain with no safe way down.

My breaths come short and shallow. Trying to breathe deeply, I tell myself I can do it. They don't baby me, and I like that, but I have to fight panic. If there's anything I've learned from trying to keep up with my brothers, it's that fear is meant to be conquered. I peek over the edge of the run. In my inexperience, it looks like a cliff. Knowing they believe in me convinces me, despite my own doubt, that I can glide down a mountain on a board.

With a steadying inhale and courage only a twelve-year-old can muster, I push off into the unknown. The air bites my cheeks as I gain speed. Before I have a chance to process the experience, the edge of my board catches and throws me to the ground. My face slams into the snow. It may look soft, but it cuts at my cheeks with razor sharpness and rattles my teeth. I stand, try again, and quickly slam back into the mountain. I glance around to see if anyone saw me fall. I shrug off my pride and try again. That irritating pattern repeats itself over and over again, until I finally reach the bottom of the run. My body is trembling, sore with fatigue. It's hard to stand, but it doesn't matter. I did it.

• • •

I conquered the mountain in my life then. Surely, I could handle the obstacles I now faced. Though the mountain was now metaphorical, I searched for a way to conquer the mountain by regaining my old life. Yet, as I tried, there were signs, big and small, that my previous life was gone.

Before I left Harborview for home, Scott brought me a teriyaki chicken wrap. I used to crave them. I'd had such a bland diet in the hospital that I couldn't wait to eat something with some kick to it. My mouth watered as I prepared for the first bite. But instead of my taste buds tingling with delight, I was repulsed. I thought something must be wrong with the wrap. It tasted nothing like I remembered. In fact, it was disgusting. How could I have ever liked it? But it wasn't the wrap that had changed; it was me. I was so fundamentally altered that even my most basic likes and dislikes were different.

The change was obvious when I met an old friend, Katherine, for lunch. She had mentored me when we worked together in Seattle, and we had become good friends. She treated me like a younger sister. I admired everything about her, from the way she stayed organized to the aerobics classes she taught.

Brie and I met her at a restaurant before an appointment to get fitted for new prosthetics. I looked forward to our meeting and imagined how it would go. But from the second I heard her voice, things were different. I couldn't get out of my wheelchair, which meant I couldn't give her a hug as I normally would have. I couldn't offer the usual "you look great" kind of comments. I knew Katherine was expecting a baby, but I couldn't see her pregnant belly. I'm sure she looked beautiful, as all pregnant women do, but as a blind person, I couldn't say that. I didn't know how to handle the conversation or situation. I wasn't the confident, competent person I wanted to be. Conversation was awkward, and so was eating. While I could feed myself, it was messy. At one point, I spilled avocado on my sleeve. I wanted to sink into the floor when Brie cleaned it off for me.

Katherine treated me with kindness and respect, as she always did. To her, the conversation was normal. It was the first time I met with someone outside my family for a social visit. It was also the first time I realized how severe my disabilities were. When it was over, I went into the restroom with Brie and cried. It wasn't that lunch hadn't gone well, but how I felt during our visit was all wrong. My illusions of returning to my former self were crushed. I wasn't the person I used to be, and I could never go back. Then came the haunting question: *If I wasn't that person, who was I?*

Throughout our meeting, I kept wondering what Katherine thought of me. I had no idea how other people perceived me. I wanted to hide my appearance by covering my physical disabilities. When someone new came to my house, I still tried to hide my legs and arm, hoping I would look normal.

One day Brie said, "Why are you hiding who you are? You can't change who you are. You need to own it."

She was right. I *did* need to own it.

It was a matter of coming to accept myself for who I was in the present rather than mourning the woman from my past. But how? How could I let go of the only life I'd ever known?

With the help of therapists, family, and friends, I looked at my life piece by piece to accept my present, which also meant letting go of my past. The first step was to give myself permission to let go of my former identity. She was gone, and no matter how much I wished for her, she wasn't coming back.

Elaine, my psychotherapist, proved key to letting go and beginning my emotional recovery. She was older, but far too hip to be any normal grandmother. She often came to my house sipping hemp milk and wearing a dragon necklace while she talked about the energy of the music that was playing. She exuded an energetic yet calming influence on those around her. Jewish by birth but Buddhist in faith, she was the right mixture of sweetness and unconventional strength to help me accept who I was. More importantly, Elaine opened herself up to me, talking about her own vulnerabilities and stories of loss. Her willingness to share of herself created a relationship of trust. That trust became a powerful tool in my therapy.

Elaine used guided meditation, as Shelly had, to help me deal with anxiety, fear, pain, and depression. Much of our time was spent looking at different parts of my life one at a time and coming to terms with them. One of her favorite sayings was, "You can't change the past, can't worry about the future; enjoy the moment and stay in the present." Through her I learned so much, but I also took an active role in my therapy. I brought issues and questions to her rather than waiting for Elaine to discover what was wrong with me—questions about my feelings surrounding my illness, disabilities, and relating to my family and friends. I put my trust and faith in her methods. With her help, I chose to stop wishing for my old life so I could live *this* life, now.

Even though I'd made the decision to let go, actually doing so proved difficult. I knew I wanted to live for Scott, Chloe, and Safiya. But everything that had defined me—snowboarding, crafts, cooking, and shopping—had changed. What hobbies could I share with my family? What could we have in common? Everything I dreamed of doing with them seemed impossible.

The more I recovered, the more questions I asked. Everything from my ability to relate to other people to what I could have done to prevent my illness came into question.

The more I focused on my past, the more stifled my present grew.

Surprisingly, looking to the future caused the same problem. As a goal-oriented person, I've always thrived on challenges. When I was home from college, I worked as a waitress at a country club. I needed more hours to pay for a car and other expenses, so I created a résumé and took it to every doctor's office in the area until someone hired me as a general gofer. I understood my end goal and took the necessary steps to achieve it. That same determination served me well during inpatient rehab, but when I looked further into the future, I was at a loss as to what kind of goals I could or should set. All I could see were my limitations. Why try to walk when I would never run with my children? Why strengthen my hand when I would never be able to hold and feed Safiya on my own? Why be present in my children's lives if I couldn't do the things a mother normally does?

The future smothered my present.

Living in the past and future prevented me from seeing my accomplishments in the present. While it's important to be mindful of the past and plan for the future, living in either one can steal the beauty of now. Looking forward could hide the joy of spending small, quiet moments with my children or Scott. For me, focusing on the tasks at hand let me see small steps of progress, which led to a subtle yet powerful change in attitude.

Feeding myself was one of the most frustrating skills I had to learn. When I took the time to take a mental step back and focused on small successes, I was able to put aside my perceived failures. While I was in inpatient rehab, I often got taco salad; it always came with two olives on top. I love olives, but they roll around. I stabbed and stabbed at my salad bowl, trying to get the olives. My dad had a hard time watching me struggle with those salads. He wanted to take the fork and stab the olives for me. It took a long time for me to eat my salad.

As much as my dad would have liked to help, I had to do it myself. I wasn't proficient at getting the olives when I left the hospital, but I kept at it for months. Finally, I got it. I could stab and eat an olive. When I reached that point, I owned it, and joy replaced frustration.

It may have been messy, but each small victory was another step toward recovery and acceptance. I felt like a toddler again, wanting everyone to know I could do it. There were setbacks and days I felt overwhelmed, but I was no longer being crushed by the past or future. Enjoying the moment allowed a new emotion to enter my life: gratitude.

Once I began to see the beauty of small moments, I realized I was able to start my life over again. I should have died from sepsis and the resulting complications, but I didn't. I got something that most people don't—a second chance. I got to start over with a lifetime's worth of experience to help me. I discovered that the best parts of me still existed and made me who I was, despite my physical limitations.

The courage it took to follow my brothers down a mountain was the same courage I needed to create a new life. I remembered being able to control my fear when following my brothers, but now I had to apply that courage when facing my disabilities. Enjoying the moment let me control fear and work past frustration.

Letting go required ridding myself of the idea of "normal." That word no longer had a place in my life. Scott and I wanted our daughters to have the usual childhood experiences. I did not want my disabilities to get in the way of their happiness. Because of that desire, I lamented the activities I would never share with them. The thought of never baking

Teaching curious friends about my disabilities.

cookies, snowboarding, or making crafts with my daughters was enough for an emotional breakdown. I didn't see how it was possible to do any of it.

Not long after I came home from inpatient rehab, Erin brought dough to bake cookies with Chloe. She knew how I felt about not being able to cook or bake with my family. The clattering of bowls, smell of flour, and Chloe's excited chatter filled the house. I sat back and listened to Safiya pounding on the table while Chloe and Erin prepared the dough.

"Come on, Carol. You're going to help roll out the dough with Chloe," Erin said.

"What? Can I do that?"

"Yup, come on." There was no hesitation in her voice. "We're making cookies today." Reluctantly I agreed, although I wasn't sure what she expected.

Sitting in my wheelchair, I tapped my fingertips against the armrest, waiting for Erin to push me to the table. I didn't want to get excited for fear it would end in disappointment. Yet, I was hopeful, even eager. Once at the table, I gently reached out my left arm toward Chloe. Her tiny hands brushed against the sensitive skin left by a skin graft as together we slowly rolled out the dough. Flour coated our limbs and a smile made its way to my face.

To my amazement, it was going well. Then, I felt a small, flour-covered finger tap my nose. I jerked and gasped in surprise.

I hadn't seen it coming, literally.

Chloe's laugh carried the pure joy of a two-year-old.

I couldn't believe it. I sat back. Was she playing with me? Were we making cookies . . . *together?*

When reality sunk in, I laughed out loud. My laughter morphed into a rejoicing of the soul. Small tears escaped my eyes, leaving happy trails on my cheeks. I shouldn't have been alive, let alone mobile and baking cookies, yet there I was in the kitchen, laughing and cooking with my daughter.

It wasn't just my eyes that hadn't seen that floury finger coming; it was my heart. A paradigm shift took place as a ray of light broke through the fog of my doubts. I could bake with my daughter. *I could be happy and not be my old self.*

An enormous weight lifted off my shoulders as I realized that so many of the things I thought were impossible might be within my reach. It was as though I had been trapped in a closed room with doors on all sides. Before baking cookies, I thought all those doors were impossible to open. I now knew I could open every one, as long as I had the resilience to try. I no

At home, playing with Chloe and Safiya.

longer saw impossible barriers but challenges to be overcome. Baking cookies acted as the catalyst I needed to get the wheels of my mind turning. Through ingenuity and imagination, I began to open more doors than I ever thought possible.

Not too many days after baking cookies with Chloe, I sat on the couch listening to Safiya wake from her nap on the baby monitor. My wheelchair didn't fit through the doorway of her room, so when I wanted to feed Safiya, someone always brought her to me as I sat in my wheelchair. But my mothering instincts were strong. I wanted to go to my baby, not have her brought to me.

Erin was always concerned about me falling when I tried to stand or walk on my own. But I knew what I had to do.

"Erin," I called. "I want to try to feed Safiya in her room. Could you get me a bottle, please?"

"Wait, you're not trying to stand, are you?" Erin answered from the kitchen.

Yes, I was.

I didn't wait for her to argue. Concentrating on balance, I pulled myself up to my walker. Each step was a move toward independence, and more importantly, toward my daughter. I was slow, but I maneuvered through the doorway and found the rocking chair in her room. I carefully sat, free and victorious.

Erin strapped the bottle into my hand brace and put Safiya in my arms. My recovery had progressed to where I could hold Safiya without severe pain to my limbs. But any discomfort at that moment would have been overshadowed by joy.

For the first time, I fed my daughter alone. In the quiet of Safiya's room, I was able to give her what she needed. *I* was needed. I imagined her tiny hands holding the bottle or waving in the air while her eyes wandered around the room taking in the colors and shapes. Gentle sucking and swallowing noises added to the peace of rocking her.

I lost myself as I stared hard in her direction, visualizing her soft hair, tiny eyelashes, and round cheeks. To my surprise, Safiya reached up and tightly grabbed my eyelashes. A shocked but happy smile spread across my face. I laughed when I couldn't get her to release me. My one hand was full of baby. She hadn't been vaguely looking around the room, as I'd imagined. She'd been looking at me—at my eyes.

When I laughed, Safiya stopped sucking to giggle. In an instant, I was her mother. It didn't matter that I couldn't get her out of the crib or prepare the bottle myself; I was still her mother. The aching grief that accompanied my inability to care for my daughter was replaced with a strong confirmation that I was hers and she was mine. Nothing could take that from me.

Bonding with Safiya was like lifting the lid to a precious gift that, until then, I hadn't known how to open.

I had to change my perception of how I would be a mother. Eliminating expectations based upon my former life allowed me to take hold of my new life. Bonding with my girls sparked an empowering sense of motivation as I continued to make physical and emotional progress. I knew I could do it. I could set goals because achieving them became about *how* to reach them rather than *if* they were possible.

Around me I had the physical tools that aided my recovery, like my walker, prosthetics, and wheelchair. But there were other tools I began to use that weren't physical, like trust in my family and therapists. Emotional healing came as I enacted tools based on faith. The same held true for my spiritual healing when I embraced gratitude and forgiveness.

To move forward, I had to let go of the mom I used to be to make room for the mom I could become. I had an epiphany baking cookies and, later, feeding Safiya, but there was still a long way to go. Starting a new life meant coming to terms with all the limitations of my condition. Gratitude was already taking a firm hold of me, but for it to become fully enmeshed in who I was, I had to forgive.

Life-altering challenges such as mine often cause a continuing cycle of bitterness, resentment, and anger. My children provided an opportunity for me to see that life held so much more than mentally dark places. For me to continue moving forward, I had to forgive myself.

A mixture of confusing emotions surrounded my illness: guilt that I wasn't there for Safiya; anger at doctors who could've done something different to prevent my disabilities;

jealousy toward the people who took care of my daughters even though I needed them to; frustration with how hard it was to do simple things. Facing my emotions helped me forgive myself and others.

I let go of the questions that had plagued me throughout my illness. Why was I alive? Why did I survive and Shawn didn't? Why did I have to suffer? I missed Shawn, and I longed to see Scott's face. Sometimes questions aren't really questions but anchors that hold us under the waters of doubt, anger, and fear. When I let go of them, I found that I became free to forgive.

As my power to forgive myself grew, so did my faith. I was able to quiet my questions and look for greater purpose. I began to weigh the thought of tragedy versus destiny. I could not control the tragedy that befell my life, but I could control my destiny. It was mine to determine by the choices I made. I chose to believe I could lead a purposeful life.

I also came to terms with the fact that there was nothing I could have done to prevent sepsis. This was huge for me. After spending countless hours asking why, forgiveness allowed me to live without the answers to those questions. I couldn't recreate the past, and trying to do so would only end in frustration and sadness. The whys of the past didn't matter, because I was living in and grateful for the present. Cutting the anchors, letting go of those questions, gave me permission to create and enjoy new experiences and memories. Once they were gone, I was free to choose who and what I wanted to be.

But forgiveness had to extend beyond myself.

I had to forgive the medical professionals who had taken care of me. I had received excellent care during my time at

Swedish and Harborview, but placing blame is a natural reaction. Forgiveness came as I chose to believe the doctors had made the best decisions they could with the knowledge they'd had at the time. Dwelling on any one decision as the cause of all my problems wasn't accurate nor did it help in my recovery. There was no one to blame. It just was.

Forgiveness freed me from the chains I had placed on myself. It was not to deny my feelings but to face them so they couldn't control me. It also allowed me to discover what emotions were "real." I'd experienced a lot of confusing emotions, many of which were caused by the heavy medications I'd taken. I, along with my therapist, was able to wade through and discover the truth versus what I had imagined. I learned that my imagination could be my own worst enemy. I imagined myself as the worst mother possible because I couldn't care for my children. Obviously, that was not true. Actual truths, such as the fact that my skin had literally been peeled from my body, had to be dealt with in a different way. I faced each problem and the accompanying emotions individually to discover the best way to move past them.

Elaine taught me to visualize. As I went through this process of discovery and forgiveness, I visualized emotional books of all sizes and colors on a mental bookshelf. Each book represented an emotion or event in my life. One at a time, we dusted off the cover of a book and examined its contents. Through this technique, I was able to face my blindness separate from my amputations, jealousy separate from anger, the loss of Shawn separate from my illness. Some books had to stay on the shelf for a long time before I was ready to look at them. Other books had to be opened before I could reach the ones that were deeper on the shelf. With each book I opened, I freed myself from the bounds placed on me by my emotions.

Forgiveness is powerful. It is liberating. It is freedom. As I strove to forgive, I could physically feel the relief as I released guilt, anger, and frustration. Acceptance and gratitude released me from my emotional chains so I could move forward to something better.

With gratitude and forgiveness, I leaped off the edge of the mountain, learning to glide down into my new life. But I also learned that life is full of mountains. Once I'd gotten over one, it didn't mean there wouldn't be more. There will always be mountains to climb and conquer. Each mountain makes me better and stronger. Each one prepares me to climb higher and overcome harder challenges. Letting go and living a life full of gratitude and forgiveness leads to a beautiful new beginning with eyes to see glorious possibilities.

CHAPTER 10

Perspective

"My mission in life is not merely to survive,
but to thrive; and to do so with some passion, some
compassion, some humor, and some style."
—*Maya Angelou*

With my heart open to the possibility of living a full life with my disabilities, there was one last part of myself I had to accept—blindness. At first, the doctors thought my vision had a good chance of returning. No one was sure why my optic nerve had stopped functioning, so they couldn't say for sure that I would never see again. Every morning I opened my eyes hoping that would be the day I would see Safiya's face. Focusing on my other disabilities let me push my blindness back to the far corners of my mind. I didn't have the ability to accept losing my feet, hand, *and* eyes at the same time.

It wasn't until I came home from the corrective surgery for my left arm and the bone spur in my leg that I was ready to take the blindness book from my mental bookshelf. Saying it out loud to Scott was the hardest part. "I'm not going to see again." Saying it made it real. "My eyes aren't coming back."

Scott wrapped his arms around me. He'd never pushed the topic, waiting until I was ready to admit it. "I'm sorry," he whispered.

"The girls. . . ." I couldn't speak what I'd known for months. I would never see Safiya walk for the first time or Chloe's first day of school. I'd functioned under the assumption that someday my vision would return. For the first time, I grieved the loss of my eyes, knowing I would never see again. Of course there were tears, but these were different. They were not hopeless or despairing but accepting. I was finally prepared to accept myself and all of my disabilities.

Without realizing it, I'd been preparing for this stage of recovery for a long time. It started when I recognized the change in my hearing while in rehab. The tone and weight of a nurse's voice could tell me she'd had a bad day, and when Erin started clearing her throat it meant she had something important to tell me. The slightest change in inflection alerted me to not only the identity of the speaker but also his or her mood.

The next steps came in close succession as my sense of touch allowed me to bond with my girls again. I couldn't get enough of them. I brought them close, cheek to cheek, so I could feel the contours of their face and kiss them with the sensitive skin of my lips. Seeing them through touch created a mental image of their faces.

The last step was opening to the idea of visualizing my surroundings. I'd started visualizing long ago in therapy, but I had only used it as a means of escape. Once I accepted my blindness, I was ready to re-create my view of the world through

At home with Safiya and Judy.

mental visualization. I no longer waited for the past but committed to the present.

I began to interact with the world as a blind person rather than a sighted person who temporarily couldn't see. I no longer *saw* the world. I tasted it. Smelled it. And felt it. Learning to see the world with my other senses was like opening a window into a darkened room. Once I became consciously aware of what I could do with my other senses, there was so much to take in I could scarcely process all of it.

The smooth surface of the kitchen counter, rough texturing of the dining room wall, and the girls playing with their toys all played a part in creating the mental picture I needed to navigate my home. I learned to feel and hear the texture of the ground with a seeing-eye cane.

Years of having eyesight helped me when I learned to visualize and recognize objects by their texture, size, and shape. But it also got in the way of progress because I knew the beauty I was missing. When Heath helped clean out my kitchen cupboards and found vase after vase from the flowers Scott had bought me over the years, I was surprised by the emotions it brought to the surface. There were far more vases than I could ever use, but as he described them to me—tall with etched flowers or round with a handle—I could picture each bouquet they'd once held: spring daffodils, lilies, or orchids.

I told Heath, "I'm never going to see a flower again."

But I was wrong.

One evening, I sat at the kitchen table talking with Erin while she made dinner when the familiar sound of fumbling keys was mixed with the distinct crinkling of plastic.

"Hey, I brought you something." Scott's keys clattered onto the counter as he greeted Erin on his way to see me.

Footsteps drew close when a powerful aroma hit me before the package he carried was placed in my arms. Breathing deeply, I recognized the rich, warm scent of roses. I traced my hand up the cellophane wrapping to the flowers.

"Could you help me pull off one of the petals?" I asked Scott.

He placed a petal between the fingers of my right hand. Bringing it to my face, I pressed its velvety surface against my lips. I couldn't stop once I'd started. I rubbed the petal across my cheek and back to my lips before I brought it closer to my nose for a deep breath. The petal against my skin and the aroma tickling my nose created a beauty I hadn't fully appreciated when I could see. Images of all the flowers I'd seen in my life flashed through my mind with vivid colors. There is more to a flower than color or shape. I had lost one kind of beauty and gained another.

Blindness changed how I saw people, too.

Sitting in a doctor's waiting room, I struck up a conversation with a woman next to me. She was hesitant to talk at first, but we soon started sharing stories about our families and eventually came around to discussing her church.

When I told her my name, she said, "I know you." Her excitement grew to a contagious level. "My church held bake sales to raise money for you and your family."

I was speechless for a minute. "You did that for me?"

"Yes. I'm so excited to meet you. You look like you're doing well."

"I am." I didn't want to let an opportunity to express my gratitude slip through my fingers. "Thank you so much for everything you and the people at your church did for me. It meant so much to us."

"You're welcome." She patted my hand. "I have just loved talking to you."

"Me too."

"You're different." She came in closer. "I'm so comfortable talking to you. I don't usually talk to other people very much."

"Really?" I didn't hide my surprise. She was such a sweet person that I couldn't imagine why she wouldn't want to talk with people.

"Yeah. I think it's because you can't see me." She hesitated, her voice lowering to a whisper. "I'm heavy. You know, overweight, really overweight. Most people don't want to talk to me. Sometimes kids stare." Her tone took a different edge, sharp, as though pained. "I don't talk much at all."

My heart ached for her and for all the people who'd missed out on knowing her innate warmth and goodness due to her

At dinner with friends.

outward appearance. In some ways, being blind lets me see clearly those things that are hidden by sight.

Without my eyes, my other senses continued to home in on the intricacies of the world around me. My hearing picked up everything with greater clarity and perception. The sound of the trees communicated what my eyes couldn't tell me. Tiny branches rustled their leaves in a light breeze, while thick branches creaked and groaned in the force of a heavy wind. Small trees whispered, while towering firs roared. From the inside of my house, the patter of rain on concrete created the same anxiety-calming cadence I'd once listened to in a hospital bed. The quiet fall of little socked feet tiptoeing into the kitchen for a treat kept me up to date on Chloe's whereabouts. Each experience, whether it was rain, wind, or Chloe sneaking to the cookie jar, became an awakening to a fresh scene I'd never thought to tap into before. Exploring sound as a blind person gave new depth to my life.

My dependence on sound led me on an insatiable quest to understand and catalogue everything I heard. I needed to know what every sound was and how it might affect me. Everything from the beep on my dishwasher to the engine of a lawn mower became important to understanding the environment around me. Learning sounds let me make decisions for myself. The better I understood everything around me, the better I was able to navigate on my own.

Now that I had a better hold of my disabilities and accepted my blindness, I was ready to welcome specialists from the Department of Services for the Blind, who'd tried to help me when I'd first come home from Harborview. I stood with a mobility specialist at a crosswalk, listening to the passing cars.

"Pay attention to the sound of the engine and how it changes as the cars get closer."

A car passed with a high-pitched whir, the sound low to the ground.

"Was that a small car?" I asked.

"Yes. What can you tell me about the next one?"

A deep rumble told me it was bigger than a car. Vibrations began to shake my body as it drew closer. It swept by, creating its own breeze, the engine deafening as it passed. "That was a truck, a big one. I think he had a lead foot."

The specialist laughed, "Good. You're right. The crosswalk is clear now. I want you to step forward and feel the ground through your prosthetic."

I leaned my foot out, trying to sense the ground beneath it. "It's sloping down."

"What else can you feel?"

I moved my foot forward a little more. "There are ridges, like bumps?"

"Those ridges are there for people like you. When you feel those, it means you're about to walk into the street."

Mobility gave me a sense of independence. After I learned to use an elevator by myself, I was eager to test my new skill. My weekly hand therapy sessions took place on the second floor of a small office building. I wanted to test my abilities by riding the elevator and arriving at my appointment on my own.

I entered the elevator and pressed the button for the second floor. Once the elevator came to a stop, I stepped out of the doors into a room with a strange, musty odor and a hum I didn't recognize. Using my seeing-eye cane, I tapped nearby. There was no plant next to the elevator or receptionist desk ahead of me. The muffled taps told me this wasn't the right floor.

Sweat beaded on my forehead. I was lost. Reminding myself to hold it together, I turned around and found the elevator doors directly behind me. When the doors opened, I took my time feeling the buttons until I was sure I was headed for the second floor. As it turns out, I'd gone to the basement. While it was scary at the time, mistakes happen. By the time I made it to my appointment, I'd found the humor in the situation and laughed as I told my therapist about my visit to the basement boiler room.

I also began working with an occupational therapist from Rehab Without Walls who had extensive experience working with the blind. She helped me develop the tools I needed to function inside my own home. I learned to use my left arm residual to feel my way through the house. I sometimes doubted what she wanted me to do, but, like my other therapists, she broadened my horizons.

"You want me to put my arm in pizza sauce?" I stood in the kitchen with Chloe and Safiya, who both sat at the table.

"Spread the pizza sauce using your left arm."

"That's gross. I'm going to get sauce all over me." Not to mention that I'd be putting my whole arm all over our food.

"Wash your hand and arm before and after," she said. I could hear the sauce slurping out of the jar as she poured. "It's not a big deal."

"Ugh." I stuck my arm in the sauce, forcing myself to ignore its cold sliminess. Chloe used a spoon to help me spread it, warning me when I got too close to the edge of the dough. As I followed a grid pattern to make sure I didn't miss a spot, cold pizza sauce spread up my arm past my elbow. Wrinkling my nose in disgust, I asked, "Is that good?"

"Yes."

I immediately went to the sink and washed my arm. All the sauce came right off. Making pizza, as it turned out, really wasn't a big deal, and I'd had fun with my kids.

Hard work and encouragement allowed me to finally take control of my daily routine. With a lot of practice and by simplifying my makeup routine, I learned to apply my own makeup. I bought eyeshadow that could be applied with my finger. I cupped the mascara wand in the crook of my left elbow and leaned my head down so I could reach my eyelashes. I replaced sponges with large-handled brushes I could hold with my right hand. Someone checked me once I was done for any mistakes.

Piece by piece my life came back into order. In many ways, I felt like a mosaic artist carefully cutting and crafting each part of my masterpiece. I was the artist changing, twisting, and altering pieces to fit. As the pieces took form they gained stability, and something beautiful began to emerge. Optimism brought on by progress and the resulting attitude change determined the shape and color of life—not my circumstances. Learning to live in the world with my disabilities let me rearrange the pieces of my life around the core of who I was, which had never changed.

I may not have liked the ache in my residuals, but I became grateful that I was alive to feel it. Feeling reminded me that there was a life to be lived. As I spent mornings talking to Chloe and listening to Safiya babble, I became more grateful for my life. Infectious optimism began to pervade our home. Embedded in the deepest recesses of my heart and mind, gratitude allowed joy to fully blossom. Being grateful changed how I saw my physical limitations. I didn't just live life; I pursued it with passion. With help from family and friends, I set goals for myself and wouldn't be deterred from achieving them. Most goals were small, but others took months of therapy and work to achieve.

• • •

"Whoa." I threw my arms out, trying to stop myself from tipping too far forward.

The prosthetist clasped my right hand, steadying my teetering body. "How do they feel?"

I let out a loud laugh. "Like I'm standing on a hill."

"Dr. Friedly didn't want you to have these. How did you get her to agree?"

I deadpanned, "I asked her at every visit until she said yes."

The prosthetist's shirt collar rustled as she shook her head. "You're sure you want to do this?"

"Are you kidding?" I took another shaky step forward on my first pair of high heels. "I said it. Now I have to do it." I moved my other foot forward and heard the satisfying clunk of my chunky heel. I'd chosen the same pair of shoes I'd worn while I was pregnant with Safiya. They seemed appropriate. Not only did they have a rubber sole with good traction, but it was Safiya's first birthday. The previous year, on that very day, my life had changed forever. Walking in those shoes was taking back another part of myself.

With a hint of amusement running through her voice, Brie added, "You aren't going to talk her out of it."

"Do you have to fit prosthetics with high heels very often?" I asked.

"Occasionally." Her voice was angled down as she stared at my feet. "Where is it you said you wanted to wear them again?"

"Wild Ginger. It's my favorite restaurant. I told Dr. Friedly I'd walk there by my next birthday. It's coming up fast, so I don't have time to waste." Another tottering step brought me closer to achieving a goal I'd been working on for months.

"Where is Wild Ginger?" Doubt clouded her usually encouraging voice.

"Downtown Seattle on Third Avenue," I said, holding my breath as I moved another leg forward.

"Up a hill," Brie added.

"Don't forget the stairs," I said. Doubt and disbelief weren't enough to stop me. If I wanted to do it, there was no time like the present. I'd already told more than one person I was going to walk in high heels again. I didn't want to let anyone down, especially myself.

Each meticulous step drained my energy but built confidence. The sway of my gait may have been different, but the Carol who strutted in her high heels was the same. As I walked down the hall on the anniversary of my illness, happiness flowed in the form of tears. Everyone in the office knew my story and shared in my achievement.

I wasn't afraid for my life anymore. I was taking it back. Accepting my blindness let me accomplish goals both big and small.

A few months later, twenty-four people came with me to Wild Ginger—my family, Scott's family, and my cadre of girlfriends. I made my way up a steep hill and stairs to the restaurant's entrance. It was nothing like my visit there the week after Shawn's funeral. Bandages no longer covered my body. I wore the slacks, blouse, jewelry, and heels that felt like me. Sampling the savory flavors and taking in the ambiance, I lived in the present. My friend Lisa cut my food for me and occasionally fed me when I struggled. The whole group stayed with me as I slowly walked back down the hill to the car.

Surrounded by the people who'd made the journey with me, I looked back on the past year. I'd reached the deepest depths of darkness and climbed high enough to radiate a happiness bright enough for others to see. I began to wonder, if so much could change in just over a year, where would I end up in another year or two or three? Possibilities filled the future.

Dr. Friedly's response was priceless when I told her I'd walked in high heels through downtown Seattle. "I thought you were crazy. I honestly didn't think you could do it," she said. I loved proving her wrong. I was ready to push the limits and test the boundaries of my new body.

Going to the grocery store, visiting the park, or walking down the street became not only ways to work on my physical therapy but adventures to share with the girls. Erin and I planned day trips, like a trip to the zoo. For most of the day, Erin pushed my wheelchair while Safiya sat on my lap. Occasionally, I walked while Chloe ran next to me, loudly announcing each animal we passed. When the sweat poured down my back, I'd take a break in the wheelchair. I rode the carousel in my wheelchair, sitting between Chloe and Safiya as they squealed. The sun shining on my face, the smell of grilled onions and hot dogs, and the fun of riding a carousel made for an unforgettable day.

Experiences became ways for me to explore my identity and continue to put myself back together. My family and friends found ways to give me the opportunities to experience life anew because they saw how it changed me.

My dad and Judy arranged a trip to a farm in rural Idaho owned by Judy's family. There was horseback riding, an ATV, and farm animals for the girls to enjoy. I'd ridden a three-wheeler as a child and couldn't wait for the freedom of bouncing over a dirt road. Greeted by open fields with the sound of irrigation systems sprinkling in the background, memories of meeting Scott in college poured through my mind.

Outside the creaky farmhouse door, my dad and I waited for a horse to be led around the house. The sound of hooves clipping on rock brought with it the feel of dust blowing against my face. I could hear the swish of the horse's tail and smell its dusty odor. Anxious at the thought of being atop an animal I couldn't see, I relied on Judy's sister and my dad to get me safely on the horse. The plan was to have me step off a low rise in the yard onto the back of the horse. That way I wouldn't have to climb a ladder.

"I'll hold the horse while your dad helps you up. Hang on with your knees," Judy's sister said.

I threw my right leg over the front of the horse, landing hard in the saddle. "Did I hit the horse with my leg?" I worried I'd clipped its ears. Usually a horse is mounted by bringing the leg over the rump, but my prosthetics wouldn't allow for that.

Judy's sister laughed and said no.

I shifted in the saddle. "How do I steer?"

"You won't need to steer. I'll lead him, but you can hang on to the reins and saddle horn if you need to."

I rocked back and forth, clinging to the saddle horn with the reins loosely looped around my hand. I gripped with my knees as I'd been told, but each step brought me dangerously close to sliding off. My feet didn't reach the stirrups, so I didn't have the leverage I needed to steady myself. It was a short ride. I'm glad I did it, but horseback riding wasn't for me.

Later that day, my dad, Judy, Chloe, Safiya, and I were riding in an ATV when my dad turned to me and asked, "Do you want to drive?" He'd used those same words when I was a child, inviting me to drive from his lap. In his typical fashion, he wanted me to have everything I wanted. I longed to be in control of a vehicle and feel the air blowing against me.

"Of course. How are we going to do it?" Faced with the real possibility, I needed to know the details of how we would pull this one off.

"Let's move you over to the driver's seat. We'll strap Chloe and Safiya in the back and you'll drive. I'll help you stay on the road."

The adrenaline started pumping. "Let's do it!"

My dad and Judy got everyone situated. When it was time to pull out, I could hardly contain my excitement. Random laughs and giggles kept bubbling out.

"Can you find the pedal?" My dad asked.

I heard the clink of metal against my prosthetic. "I'm pushing it now, right?" The pedal pushed my foot back at me.

"That's it. I'm going to take the brake off." My dad was almost as excited as I was. "You ready?"

"Okay, so I just keep the steering wheel straight?" I rubbed my hand over the steering wheel, feeling its power in my hand. We started slow, barely creeping forward. I followed my dad's instructions without hesitation as we made a circle. I straightened out the wheel while we idled.

"I think you've got it. You ready to go faster?"

Tingles moved through my body. "Yes."

"You've got a straight dirt road ahead of you." He leaned in closer. "Go like hell."

He released the parking brake, and we tore down a bumpy road at the side of a field. I jerked left and right. We probably went faster than we should have, but I strictly followed my dad's commands. An occasional slam on the brakes brought all of us to a lurching halt. Chloe and Safiya squealed with delight in the back seat, yelling at the cows as we passed or screaming a hello to the dogs when we came near the house.

After an hour we picked up Judy's eighty-year-old dad to give him a ride, too. The stress of riding with a blind driver with a taste for speed was too much for him. He lasted only a few minutes before exclaiming, "Get me out of here!"

For two hours, freedom was mine. Speed, screaming, thrills. It was glorious.

My dad finally informed me, "We'd better get back to the house. It's getting late. We can go back through the fields, but that will take a while. The fastest way back is on the county road."

"Is anyone coming on the road?" I asked, the tingles coming back again.

"Nope." He knew which I would choose but left the decision up to me.

The road had been clear of traffic all afternoon. It seemed like an ideal opportunity. "Then let's take the fast road."

The steering smoothed as we pulled over the crackling gravel onto the paved road. We hadn't been on the road for long when my dad started to laugh.

"There's a truck coming up on your left." There was a note of warning in his voice even though he couldn't stop chuckling. "Stay calm, don't change anything. We should pass right by, and he'll never know he drove past a blind woman."

"Okay. Tell me when we get close and I'll wave." I held tightly to the steering wheel with my right hand, preparing my left arm for a wave.

"Now, he's right in front of us!"

I threw my lucky fin in the air, frantically waving at the driver as though we were old friends. My family and I still laugh about that day and the poor driver who didn't know he shared the road with a blind triple amputee.

The thrill of living filled that afternoon, and I got to share it with Chloe and Safiya.

Pushing boundaries had always been a part of my personality. I found that having disabilities didn't change my need to test limits. Riding in the ATV was an experience that helped me understand who I was and what I could do.

Over time, my life and identity kept taking shape as I continued to learn and experience the world in my new body. I pursued life rather than letting it happen to me. Instead of dreading my future, I couldn't wait to see what it held.

Finding and understanding my identity was a continual process that helped me be a better mom for Chloe and Safiya. Part of that desire to go and do new things came from wanting to share life experiences with them. I wanted to do normal things like taking them to a pumpkin patch. With the help of my physical therapist and Erin, we made it happen.

The pumpkin patch was an intense therapy session in which I tested my balance and endurance. At the same time, I got to share the experience with Chloe and Safiya.

My therapist held my arm as I stumbled through a muddy field dodging vines, pumpkins, and kids. I used my seeing-eye cane while Erin kept Chloe and Safiya nearby. I couldn't keep the smile from my face as Chloe and Safiya ran circles around us. The smell of wet hay and straw permeated the air as the girls jumped in a barn full of corn kernels, held kittens, and chose the perfect pumpkins. We took a break late in the afternoon to eat fresh donuts and drink hot chocolate. My tired, aching muscles were ready to sit down and rest. The girls couldn't stop talking about how many pumpkins they could see and asking if we could come back the next year. My exhaustion couldn't outweigh my happiness, and it's a tradition we've kept every year since then.

The beauty of that day wasn't complete until we'd begun to make our way to the car. Picking my way through the parking lot with my therapist, another mom stopped us.

She spoke directly to me. "Excuse me? Can I ask you a few questions?"

I didn't wait for my therapist or Erin to answer. "Sure."

"We went to the library for the blind in Seattle last week. Can my daughter and I ask you a few questions about your cane?"

I answered her questions with a growing admiration. Most people taught their children not to stare, with the unintended consequence of ignoring the disabled. This mother wanted her daughter to know and understand, not be afraid. I was thrilled to tell her why and how I used my cane. I thanked her for taking the time to teach her daughter.

Talking to that mom and her daughter was the first time I understood my ability to educate and affect the lives of others by talking about my disabilities. I realized I could make a difference. Not only that—I *wanted* to make a difference. At the time I didn't know what I would do with that desire, but talking about my disabilities was therapeutic and empowering. It would still be some time before I realized the purpose that would enter my life because of my disabilities.

In the meantime, my confidence in my abilities grew to

the point that I wanted to do things on my own. When Chloe entered preschool, I wanted to participate in her school activities like other moms. I was determined to attend her first class party. I didn't want Chloe to be the only one without her mother there.

Erin got me situated in a chair along the wall, worry filling every movement she made. "Are you sure you don't want me to stay?"

"I'll be okay." This was something I wanted to do on my own. "Thanks."

With a heavy sigh, she said, "Okay. Safiya and I will be back in an hour and a half."

Chloe had already rushed off to play with her friends while her teacher explained an activity. I listened and waited. Other moms sat a few chairs away, but no one sat next to me. They struck up conversations with one another about their kids and other normal "mom" conversations.

No one spoke to me. No one sat next to me. Maybe I'd made a mistake. I wondered if I was wrong to send Erin away. For a minute, I imagined the other parents staring at me while I sat in silence. Then, I thought of Chloe. This wasn't for me; it was for her. If I wanted them to talk to me, I was going to have to break into the conversation. I remembered the mother from the pumpkin patch. Not all parents were like her, but I believed the other moms weren't being cruel. They just didn't know how to include me.

When I heard a woman near me ask, "What shows do your kids like to watch?"

I chimed in, "Chloe likes *Wonder Pets*. Have you guys seen that one?"

There was silence—maybe a little surprise that I'd said anything. Then one of the moms said, "Yes, with the duck and guinea pig?"

"Yes. They're so cute," I added.

"We have to make a trip to the pet store every time we watch it," another said as she laughed.

With a small effort, I'd become part of the group. I had to put myself out there and show them I wanted to be a part of the conversation. Once I did, they included me as they would have anyone else. There was a time in my recovery when I wouldn't have showed up at the party, let alone joined in the conversation. When I worked as a medical assistant, I developed the skills to put people at ease. The skills were still there, but I had to remember how to use and apply them in the situations in which I found myself.

My comfort in talking to people and sharing my experiences with sepsis and disabilities led to new opportunities I'd never anticipated. I was asked to speak at a small conference for young women ages twelve to eighteen and their mothers. The theme of the evening was "I Can Do Hard Things." I knew I could do hard things, but I wasn't sure I could relate my message to teenage girls.

My typical insecurities reemerged. What would I say? What if they couldn't relate to me? What if something embarrassing happened?

I knew I could offer honesty, gratitude, and perspective. I hoped that sharing my story would change their lives. In a way, sharing my story was my way of offering service, something I didn't get to give very often.

My message centered on the image of a rock—something

simple but solid and immovable, like faith and family. I told them having a solid foundation lets you make something good out of something bad. I taught them that it came down to choices. Tragedy and sadness could swallow happiness if they let it. I encouraged them to choose good. To choose a life of purpose. To choose gratitude and to appreciate who they were. Through all of that, I shared my story of loss and heartache, but I also shared the joy I'd found in being a wife and mother. Even though tears poured down my cheeks, calm filled the room.

That night, my illness served a special purpose. My journey touched the hearts of those young women and their mothers. As time went on, I was asked to speak at more events. Many times, members of the audience would share their losses with me, but they shared their hope as well. If I could reach only one person each time I spoke, it was worth it. I could change lives. My greatest joy will always come from being a mother, but serving others by sharing my story gave my long months of suffering greater purpose.

I'd come to a place in my journey where it didn't matter what had happened in the past, because the present was worth living. Goals had been a way to keep myself going while I slogged through the hardest days of rehab, but goals led to experiences and opportunities that propelled me in a direction I had never anticipated.

CHAPTER 11

Strap on Your Gear and Go

*"Life is a gift. If you don't open it, you'll
never experience the beauty inside."*
—*Carol J. Decker*

The final step in my recovery was to go forward and enjoy living. Little by little I grew stronger and bolder in
my goals and pushed boundaries with a willingness to try.
Opportunities continued to open as I gained skills and became
equipped with the right gear.

Prosthetics completely altered the possibilities available to
me. They gave me freedom, but they also weighed me down.
My first pair felt like ankle weights that took energy to both put
down and pick up. It was an exhausting way to navigate, as my
feet didn't spring off the ground as a natural foot would. A walk
around the block left me panting, sweating, and ready to sleep
for hours. I would replace an old pair after surgeries or as they
began to wear out, and each new pair required an adjustment to
the fit and feel. For long distances, I still had to use a wheelchair.

But Greg Davidson, an innovative prosthetist, changed my world. He modified Cheetah Legs, a prosthetic design for runners, for everyday use. I'd been using prosthetics for a few years by the time I tried my first pair of Cheetah Legs.

I sat in his office, snapping the legs on myself. I hesitated before I stood, hoping these legs would be different. I'd heard great things about Cheetah Legs but kept my expectations realistic.

"Stand up nice and slow." I could feel Greg's presence close by as I stood.

I waited for the feel of a heavy weight at the end of my legs. As soon as my full weight was on the prosthetics, a strange sensation went through my entire body. Even standing, I could tell these legs were unlike any I'd tried before.

"Wow," I said. I fought the desire to bounce on them like a trampoline.

"Are you ready to walk?"

One cautious step after another, I moved forward. The Cheetah Legs responded to my every command, springing me onward like a diving board. There was no lumbering drag or weight holding me down. Every bump and dip of the floor made its way from the prosthetics to my body. Within five steps, I knew these legs would change everything. As I continued to walk, I tried to say, "These are incredible," but I couldn't get the words out. I put my hand to my mouth to hold back my emotions.

"Thank. . . ." Words still wouldn't come. I stopped moving to cover my face. These prosthetics felt like me. They propelled my body forward. They moved me toward freedom. The possibilities were endless. Sniffles filled the room.

Portrait at home.

Even Greg struggled to keep his emotions under control. "So you like them?"

"They are incredible, Greg." How do you express the gratitude of being given the ability to not just walk but move freely? His work changed everything. Mobility would let me do more for and with my girls. There was nothing more important than that. "I love them."

We worked our way down the hall to a ramp. I could sense the curvature and angle of the floor with each step. As I made my way around his office, I pictured keeping up with my growing girls and walking them to school one day. I couldn't stop thanking him.

His voice thick with happiness and satisfaction, he said, "This is one of the greatest moments of my career."

With good reason, my reactions were different than most patients. As a blind person, I was more sensitive to how the Cheetah Legs *felt*. I had no visual cues to warn me about the terrain, so everything I experienced came from how the legs functioned. Greg questioned me extensively, trying to understand exactly what worked and what didn't. I also didn't guard my emotions the way a seeing person would. I couldn't see people's reactions to my emotions, which oddly enough made me more open and free when expressing what I felt.

Cheetah Legs expanded the possibilities. Eventually, the time came when we didn't need Erin's help anymore. She could retire for real. Before I was ready for that change, I made her time how long it would take me to get Chloe and Safiya out of the house by myself during a fire. I didn't ever want my disabilities to put the girls in danger. With or without my Cheetah Legs, I wanted to be prepared.

I popped open windows and helped the girls out onto the grass, pulling myself out last. The thrill of my accomplishment was outweighed by the realization that I'd forgotten to unlock the front door. I also learned to get back into my house in an emergency.

Life as a blind triple amputee could be scary at times, but I chose not to let fear dictate the course of my life. Instead, I imagined the possibilities. When my dad and Judy started talking about a family trip to Hawaii, I was all in. Scott, on the other hand, was a bit wary.

"I've called the airline." He tapped a pencil on the table. "They told me they'll have a wheelchair waiting when we get off the plane."

"People use wheelchairs in the airport all the time. I'm sure it's going to be fine." My heart pounded thinking about it, but there was no way to get over the anxiety unless we faced it.

I heard Scott run his hand over his face. "I know, but I want to know how things are going to go down. I don't want to be caught off guard."

Flying to Hawaii was full of unknowns. Chloe and Safiya hadn't been on a plane before, and the flight to Hawaii would take five hours. I didn't know how my amputated limbs would do on a long flight. And, of course, there was the question of getting me through security with prosthetics and our luggage.

Scott's careful planning left us plenty of time to get to the airport in case there were unexpected delays. All was well until we hit security.

"Ma'am, we can take you to the front of the line. Then we'll need to do a full pat-down." I didn't argue. I'd expected as much with all my gear. When they said full pat-down, they meant a *full* pat-down. Every part of me was searched from head to toe. Luckily, I was so used to being touched and handled from all my time in the hospital that it didn't bother me. I couldn't take my shoes off the prosthetics, so the agents carefully wiped down my shoes to check them while Scott waited with the girls on the other side.

Five minutes later, I heard, "You're free to go, ma'am. Thank you for your cooperation." Just like that, we were ready to board the plane.

As Scott grabbed the handles of my wheelchair, he said, "Well, that wasn't as bad as I thought it would be."

The flight, too, was uneventful, leaving me time to visualize the Hawaiian beaches. I couldn't wait for the girls to play in the sand and water. Ideas began popping up in my mind

*At home doing what I love best, snuggling
with my girls, Chloe and Safiya.*

from the minute we arrived. I thought of activities to do with
the girls, but I also wanted Chloe and Safiya to see me pushing
myself to try new things.

The heat of the Hawaiian sun added to the myriad sensations of the beach. The sand and water felt different on my
grafted skin, but I soaked it all in. Chloe and Safiya's happy
screams broke through the thick tropical air. They'd run to the
water and then back to me, bringing with them the smell of
sunscreen mixed with ocean.

I took off my prosthetics before I entered the water clinging to Scott's back. I could feel the raw power of the open
water churning around me. It swirled and touched every part

Decker family photo.

of my skin. I wore a flotation device that Scott and my dad took turns hanging on to so I didn't float out to sea. The girls swam between me and the shore. Bobbing with the waves and listening to my children play was paradise.

Not only did I get to experience Hawaii in a new body, I got to experience it through my children. Fire dancers and roasted pig at an evening luau had them amazed. In their excitement, they described it all to me, trying to help me see it through their eyes. The taste of fresh pineapple and air scented with exotic flowers created an almost intoxicating atmosphere.

While there, I looked for ways to push myself beyond my limits.

"I want to try getting on a surfboard," I told Heath.

By this time, no one was surprised by my ideas. Scott, my dad, and Heath were the ones who rarely doubted I'd be able to do the things I wanted. With his usual enthusiasm, Heath replied, "Let's figure it out, then."

I floated next to Heath while he and my dad held either side of the board. My dad helped me climb on, laying me down on my stomach.

Rising and falling with the water, I took a deep breath, "I think I'm ready."

"Get on your hand and knees first," said Heath. "I'll keep the board as still as I can."

"Okay." Quick, nervous breaths came out with the effort it took to balance. On hand and knees, I did it. At one point, I knelt up on my knees with my arms stretched out for balance.

"I'm going to let go," Heath said.

He released the board and, for a brief moment, I was alone on the board, moving with the waves.

"This is amazing!" I called to Heath just before I lost my balance and slammed into the water. I got back on and crashed several more times.

Who could have imagined that a few years after losing my feet, hand, and sight that I would be on a surfboard in Hawaii? Each new experience became a step forward on the path I had started when I left inpatient rehab. The further along I went, the less I cared about a destination, because new experiences were everywhere.

A few months after I went to Hawaii with my family, my close friend Erica was going to travel to Barbados for her birthday. She planned to go alone, but extended an invitation to me, declaring it would be an adventure for us both. Erica and I lived hundreds of miles apart, but I wanted to go. To make it happen, I would have to fly the first leg of the trip by myself.

Scott was beside himself with worry, planning every portion of the trip down to the minutest detail. He didn't want anything to go wrong while I was on my own. I won't lie: I was nervous. But I was determined to go even if others tried to dissuade me.

I do not drive or go anywhere by myself. But this was a chance to do something big on my own. *I* would have to take care of any problems along the way. The flight was scheduled for November fifth, the same day I'd left inpatient rehab years before.

Scott insisted I fly first class to be sure I got extra care. Once on the plane, I kept checking my seat belt and feeling for my backpack. The man sitting next to me asked where I was going.

"Barbados."

"Barbados is amazing." His voice carried an open friendliness I instantly liked. "Have you been before?"

"No, this is my first time." I gave my seat belt another tug.

His voice rose, accentuating an undercurrent of shock. "You're going by yourself?"

"Not exactly. For this leg of the flight, yes. I'm meeting a friend partway, and we'll fly down together."

"Good for you." Our conversation fell into a quick and easy friendship as he gave me insider tips and tricks for at least an hour about vacationing in Barbados.

"How does a woman like you end up flying to Barbados with a friend?" He finally asked.

I wondered when he'd get around to my disabilities. I was more than happy to share with him. I told him about sepsis, Safiya's birth, amputations, and grafting. The flight was long enough that I went into detail about rehab. We even talked about Shawn. He asked a few questions, but it was already time for our plane to land.

As the click of seat belts began to fill the plane, my new friend lightly touched my arm. "I wish I had what you have." He rummaged under his seat while I pondered what he'd said. It wasn't the first time I'd heard those words.

After I'd gathered my things, he asked, "Can I take a picture with you?"

"Sure."

He held his camera in front of us. "Am I looking in the right direction?" I asked. The click of the button told me I must have been.

"Close enough." He paused with his hand on my arm, "Would you allow me the honor of walking you to meet your friend?"

Somewhat taken aback, gratitude welled within me. "I would love that."

I held his arm as we made our way off the plane. He delivered me safely to a curious Erica. I introduced him before thanking him for his help.

"It has been my pleasure, Carol." With that he was gone, and I never saw him again.

It was the perfect beginning to the trip.

Erica helped me get my seeing-eye cane out while I got my backpack and suitcase situated. As we began walking, I played out scenarios in my mind, like dropping my suitcase and having it fall open or tripping and falling on a ramp. I was busy working out how I would fix potential problems. Then, I stopped and listened to the hum of people in the airport. Any one of them could drop a suitcase or trip. They would pick themselves up and keep going. I calmed my nerves by recognizing that I would do the same as anyone else. My worry subsided as we continued our slow progress through the airport.

A fluid wall of heat and humidity welcomed us in Barbados. Heat waves bounced off the tarmac, creating a sheen of sweat all over my body as soon as we stepped off the plane. Grafts and prosthetics make temperature adjustments complicated. Grafted skin cannot sweat, and the protective layers I wore underneath my prosthetics trapped my body heat. But I wasn't going to let the heat ruin this opportunity.

One of our most memorable day trips was in a catamaran to go snorkeling with other tourists. Erica jumped in the water at the first stop, snapping photos with her underwater camera while I listened to the slap of waves against the boat. At the next stop, I moved closer to the edge to be near the action. In the tropical heat, the water sounded so soothing. A familiar itch to swim must have shown on my face. Wiping my sweaty forehead, I was startled by a man's voice behind me. "Would you like to get in the water?" I recognized the friendly voice as the guide who had greeted us when we got on the boat.

"I would love to, but I can't do it myself."

"My name is Raymond." A kind hand rested on my elbow. "If you would like, I can swim with you?"

"Yes, that would be great."

He and Erica helped me into the water. He asked permission before placing his hands on me and made sure to tell me before he did anything. The next thing I knew I was floating with my new friend Raymond in the waters surrounding Barbados.

"To your right is a bright blue fish with yellow fins. He is mischievous, darting through the coral. A large sunfish is passing underneath you right now. If you hold still, you might feel it brush against you."

"This is amazing," I told him. He described everything in detail so I could clearly picture it. Erica swam around us, getting pictures to show Scott. Raymond held me until it was time to move to the next stop.

At the last snorkeling area, I spoke with another tourist who was there with her two friends. I learned that the three of them traveled the world together.

"When my friends and I travel, they snorkel while I stay in the boat." Conviction and a change in perspective filled her words. "I watched you swim. I'm not staying in the boat next time. I'm going to snorkel like everyone else." It was her turn to experience life.

"You just have to go for it. You won't regret it," I told her.

As we sat on the boat making our way to the shore, another woman said to me, "You have perspective."

"Yes," I said, the breeze blowing my hair behind me. "How did you know?"

Her voice was eerily perceptive and honest. "You know that life is worth living. I have perspective, too. I survived breast cancer. I'm cancer free, and I'm here to celebrate."

I knew exactly how she felt. "My life started over once too. Life *is* worth celebrating."

Yes, it is.

Walking my girls to school, having lunch with a friend, laughing with Scott at the end of a long day are the small moments of a beautiful life worth celebrating. The big events punctuate the daily journey we share together.

Sharing that joy and purpose with my girls has always been important to me. I want them to know who I was before sepsis because, while that person is gone, she is still a vital part of who I have become. I've had to search for ways to share the things I love with them.

The idea of snowboarding with Chloe and Safiya wouldn't leave my mind no matter how I tried to tell myself it would be impossible. I needed to get back on a mountain. I could still hear the sound of a snowboard cutting through fresh powder. The freedom and speed were something I had to pursue. I needed it for my girls so they would know who I was before sepsis. They needed to see my passion and drive. And I needed it for me—to know I hadn't given up on something I loved.

Five years after I had Safiya, I pulled out a final piece of my former life, no longer satisfied with the *idea* of snowboarding. I made a goal to go to the mountain again. Doubts were set aside as I searched for ways to make it happen. That's when I found Outdoors for All, a company that develops outdoor equipment and opportunities for people with disabilities. Without hesitation, I signed up for a six-week course. Riding up with Heath to the mountain on a cold January night, I shifted in my seat and tapped my fingers on the door, knowing I couldn't go back on my crazy idea.

I sat in the ski patrol building listening to volunteers explain a sit-ski. A sit-ski has a chair with two skis underneath it. My legs rested on a platform out in front. Seat belts tightened over my ankle, knees, and hips. My arms fit into outriggers for steering. My left arm had to be duct taped to stay in place.

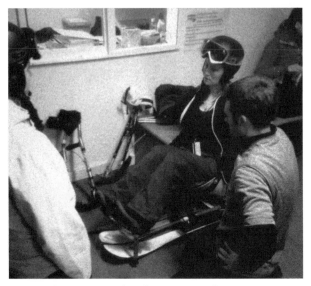

Achieving my goal and returning to the mountain.

During training, the chair was attached by a rope to a skier behind me, with skiers on each side for safety.

"Now we've got all your equipment on," the volunteer's words slurred in the cold air, "we're going to head over to the bunny hill so you can get a feel for the skis."

"Bunny hill?" My pride prickled. "Can't we just go up the lift and do an easy run?"

Heath chuckled.

In all seriousness, the guide replied, "We want to make sure you are comfortable and have some control before we go up the mountain."

I suppose I could see the wisdom of that policy, but I didn't start snowboarding on a bunny hill. Apparently, they don't follow the Heath and Shawn method of teaching.

"I guess you're right. Let's do this."

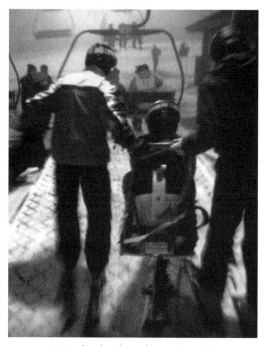

Excited to head out for another ride.

Even on the bunny hill, the pull of the snow on the skis sent chills up my back. This was me. Memories of snowboarding trips with my brothers flooded through my mind's eye. I couldn't dwell on them too much, because I needed to listen. Leaning with my body and pushing with my arms, I began making lazy turns. It looked and felt different, but the joy was not.

"That went well," my guide said. "You've got pretty good coordination and control. Do you think you're ready for the lift and a real run?"

"Yes!" I could hardly believe he would ask me that question.

The ski lift posed a different kind of challenge. Chairlifts move constantly to keep as many people moving up the hill as possible. Two people would have to lift me into the seat while the lift slowed to a stop. My heart skipped a few beats as I rose in the air. It completely thumped out of my chest when they lifted me so high that the back of my skis caught on the chairlift, flipping me upside down.

I didn't fall out of the sit-ski but dangled with my arms in the air. In the meantime, the operator stopped the chairlift while skiers and snowboarders piled up in line. Having been stuck in a lift line myself, I knew people were probably getting cranky.

"I'm so sorry," one of the volunteers immediately said. "Get that other side and let's flip her." They flipped me and moved me over to the side so the lift could continue.

Upright and slightly embarrassed, I could feel the mortification emanating from my guides. I could picture what I must have looked like hanging upside down while strapped to a chair, skis waving skyward. I couldn't help but start laughing.

My guides remained silent. I'm sure they thought I was trying to cover my true feelings. I wasn't. If I wanted a successful run, I was going to have to put them at ease. "Okay, guys," I said through my laughter. "What happened back there was like the worst-case scenario. I'm glad we got it out of the way. Let's have some fun."

They chuckled a little but maintained the serious work of getting me on the chairlift.

Getting off the lift required some maneuvering, but we managed to do it without another bottoms-up. We pushed off and never looked back. Before I knew it, the biting January air blew my hair back, stinging my eyes and taking my breath away. I can only describe it as bliss—a place where worries couldn't exist.

Valentine's Day of that year, Scott and the girls came with me to my ski lesson for the first time. I could control my speed and turn well enough to carve my way down a slope. I would always need help getting on and off the lift, but accepting help is part of living with disabilities.

Fresh powder covered the mountain. Each turn was like cutting through clouds. As Chloe and Safiya rode the chairlift with me, I made sure to absorb everything—the excitement in their voices, their descriptions of the run beneath the lift, the way their wiggling bodies made the chair swing. The sweetness of it sank deeply into my memory. It was as though my heart swelled, threatening to break out of my chest with the love and gratitude I felt.

All day the girls rushed by me, calling, "Hi, Mommy!"

It was perfection.

I weaved my way down the mountain with Scott and the girls nearby while my guides kept me and other skiers safe. But just like any normal skier, I caught an edge and took a fall in the snow. My sit-ski lay on its side with me safely strapped inside. I lay motionless in the powder. My guides rushed over to make sure I was okay.

"I'm so good right now," I laughed. "Can you leave me here for just a minute? This feels amazing."

Lying in the soft powder was the perfect end to the day. I didn't have to concentrate on my arms or body. I could listen to the cut of skis as they passed by, feel the growing cold of the snow, and hear voices as they disappeared down the run. My heart and soul were complete. I could have died right then and been satisfied knowing I'd done all that I'd set out to do.

How many times had I heard I might not make it? How

many times had I wondered if I would reach another birthday or be there for Chloe's first day of school? There was no question anymore. All the work, heartache, and sacrifice were worth that moment.

Riding home in the car, I told Scott, "This is the best Valentine's Day ever. I know it should be about us, but it's not."

We had made it—our marriage, our girls, our family, and me.

I'm so grateful for companies like Outdoors for All and the many volunteers that make special moments possible for disabled people. They give hope and make dreams come true for people who are limited by their own bodies. Later that year, when Outdoors for All asked me to be part of their yearly fund-raiser, I was honored and privileged to do anything I could to promote their programs.

Each year they choose one person to highlight at their fund-raiser to use as an example of what their programs can accomplish. They filmed a short documentary showing how I used a sit-ski. I got to try out some of their other equipment as well, my favorite being a tandem bike.

The night of the fund-raiser, my mom made sure I looked my best. "You've got to hold still," she said as she fluffed, smoothed, and sprayed my hair.

"Sorry," I said without a hint of remorse. "I can't believe this is happening."

"I'm almost finished." With a few final tugs and tucks, she declared me ready to go.

"Is everything on my dress straight? Nothing is showing that shouldn't be?" Errant pieces of underclothing, without my knowledge, had been known to peek out. I couldn't have that happening on this special night. I reached up to feel my hair and received a light tap on the head.

"Don't touch your hair," my mom scolded.

I laughed. She'd been telling me that since I was a little girl.

"You look beautiful," she added. Knowing my mom might be a little biased, I made sure to get a couple more opinions before we went into the fund-raiser. The extra attention from my mom, Heath, and Scott, along with the silky dress I wore, made me feel like royalty.

The conference center was filled with people with disabilities and potential donors. Being in a room full of people like me was like coming home. We naturally understood one another despite the differences in our disabilities. I sat with my family at the head table, nervously going over the speech I'd prepared in my head.

My documentary ended to applause. Nervous and shaking, I went to the podium to deliver my speech, thanking the company and all they had done, as well as everyone who was there to raise money. The speech I'd so carefully prepared was interrupted by my own tears. How could I speak when there was so much to be grateful for—experiences, friends, family, my very life. Scott and I stayed onstage while the bidding started. As the money kept coming in, I couldn't believe the generosity with which so many people gave. Over half a million dollars was raised that night.

At the end of it all, Scott and I sat at our table greeting other guests who wanted to share their story or shake my hand.

Scott suddenly said, "Hey, I know that guy." Scott's voice was turned away from me as though he were searching the crowd.

"Where do you know him from?"

"I'm not sure, but he and his wife are coming to our table."

I waited while Scott thought.

"Carol, I know who he is." Scott's voice had fallen to a hushed tone. "It's Dr. Solomon."

"Dr. Solomon from Swedish?" Dr. Solomon was one of the first doctors who had treated me at Swedish Medical Center. He'd been the one to tell Scott about sepsis. Throughout my stay at Swedish, he'd checked in and watched over my progress. My family often talked about his kindness and concern during the early stages of my illness.

"Yes." Scott scooted his chair back and reached out his hand.

I fell back in my chair, clutching my chest. Shock covered my face. I was there that night in part because of Dr. Solomon's efforts so long ago. Early in my recovery, his decisions had kept me alive.

Dr. Solomon introduced himself and his wife. I couldn't speak. I sat there stunned. Finally, I forced myself to stand and face him.

"Dr. Solomon," I said reaching out my arms. "How can I ever thank you?" Putting my arms around his neck, I left a kiss on his cheek. More tears streamed down my face as I uttered "thank you" and kept hugging him. I couldn't stop. I felt so much gratitude, and nothing I did seemed like enough to tell him how much he meant to me. I was not only thanking him but all of the people who'd helped me survive along the way. There were so many who truly cared and sacrificed on my behalf.

His voice was choked. "After you left Swedish, I didn't know if you'd survived. I never got word."

While Dr. Solomon and I hugged, his wife spoke with

Scott. "When he was treating her, he used to come home and agonize over what to do. He cried at night worrying. Even though he did everything he could, he didn't know if she'd make it."

"I made it," I told him through tears and a happy laugh. "Did you know I was going to be here tonight?"

"I had no idea. My wife works in pediatrics with children who use this program, so we were here for the fund-raiser. When I saw the video, I couldn't believe it."

I had to tell him everything—Chloe, Safiya, and my work as a speaker. I wanted him to know that I was making the best of the life I'd been given.

I'm often asked, if I could go back and change things, would I?

Without hesitation, the answer is—no.

The mother I have become, the people I have met, and the experiences I have had could have come to me in no other way. I wouldn't change a thing.

Some of the greatest gifts in this life come from adversity. We can choose joy despite our circumstances. I *choose* to live in light. To taste, smell, hear, and touch all that is good and make it part of myself. I've navigated troubled waters, and I know they can be calmed. Though my body may be broken, the spirit inside is not. Trials and heartache have made me stronger despite my physical limitations.

If the journey behind me is any indication of what is to come, more challenges are ahead. But I know there is joy to be found because—

I choose a beautiful life.

Acknowledgments

I am truly one of the luckiest girls alive. As far as giving thanks to all who have helped with this book, thank you to everyone at Shadow Mountain for all of your time and hard work. I would especially like to thank Michelle Wilson, Stacey Nash, and Chris Schoebinger for collaborating with me and making this book happen. Thank you, Michelle, for being my mentor and cheerleader. To Stacey, thank you for giving my story elegance and grace. I'm so grateful for the connection we have and friendship we've developed. And Chris, thank you for your genuine acceptance and kindness.

Words cannot express the love I have for everyone who has supported and loved me through my life and especially the tragedy of sepsis. I will be forever grateful to all of the medical staff at Swedish Hospital, Harborview Medical Center, Harborview Inpatient Rehab, Rehab Without Walls, Good Sam Outpatient Rehab, the Department of Services for the Blind, and all other medical staff who supported and helped me through the recovery process to start my new life. Thanks to Dan Steel for providing additional physical therapy and pushing me beyond my limits. Thank you to Greg Davidson for making me the most incredible legs so I could be a better mom.

Thank you to Outdoors for All. You made skiing with my family a reality. I am so grateful that I got to be a part of your fund-raiser. You made my dreams come true.

Thank you to the entire Enumclaw community for supporting me with your generosity, including monetary gifts, food, prayers, notes, and cards. Thank you for organizing the fund-raiser. You truly made me feel like I had a giant cheering section rooting for me!

Thank you to the Enumclaw wards of The Church of Jesus Christ of Latter-day Saints for uplifting my spirit with all of your prayers, fasting, and well wishes. Thank you for providing meals for my family for the first two years after I came home from the hospital. Also, a big thank you to members of the Church worldwide who prayed and fasted for me and my family.

I would like to thank everyone in my hometown of Kennewick, Washington, for their love, support, and fund-raisers. I would also like to thank everyone who commented on Scott's blog. It truly uplifted me and helped me to remember I was important.

To all of my friends who believed in me and made me feel like I was important no matter what. Again, I am forever grateful for all of your sincere friendship and love through the years.

To my dearest angel in disguise, Erin Rose Stout, AKA Nanny, thank you for being by my side every day for the first four years of my recovery. You have seen me at my worst and my best. There is no way I could've done this without you. Thank you from the bottom of my heart for loving my two beautiful daughters like your own grandchildren. You are part of my family, and I love you always!

Thank you to the Decker family. You have always welcomed me with open arms. I love all of you so much, and I couldn't have done this without your help. Thank you for supporting Scott in any capacity that he needed when I couldn't. That means the world to me. I will be forever indebted to you. Special thanks to Scott's parents, Kent and Joanne Decker, for the unconditional love you have given me. I feel honored to be your daughter-in-law. Thank you for raising the most incredible man and teaching him to be the person he is. I am so proud to call him my husband, and I love you dearly.

To the Vance and Baddley families, I am so thankful and appreciate all of the many things you have done for me. I feel so privileged to call you my family. I love all of you.

To Dad, thank you for teaching me to be resilient, for always believing in me, and pushing me to work hard. Most especially, thank you for letting me know I am truly loved. And to Judy, my stepmother, thank you for loving me when you didn't have to. Thank you for loving my girls and taking care of them when I could not. It meant the world to me. Your support through my hardest times helped me regain my new life. I miss and love you dearly. I'm sorry you're not here to see this book come to fruition. Thanks to Mandy, my stepsister, for always making me feel welcome and a part of your family.

To my amazingly strong mother, who is my bright shining star that I have always looked up to. You have so much grace and beauty and so many talents and gifts. Thank you for teaching me to be kind and compassionate to others. I am truly honored to be your daughter, and I can never thank you enough. I can hardly express the gratitude and love I have for you. Every day, I give thanks that you are my mother. You are the best!

To my devoted big brother Heath, who gave up his life to be by my bedside every day in the hospital, you have always made me feel important and loved. Thank you for teaching me to be fearless and brave. I am always overwhelmed with emotion when I think of all the things you have done for me. I have always been able to depend on you because of your loyalty. You are my hero, and one of the most extraordinary people I know. Thank you so much for being you. I love you always.

Finally, I would like to thank my amazing little family. Scott, from the moment I laid eyes on you, I fell in love with you. You are so handsome, smart, and talented. You are one of the most generous people I know. The love I have for you is indescribable. You are my eternal soul mate. You have given me my life back and have done everything in your capacity to help me be the successful person I am today. I always knew how wonderful you were. Now you have shown the world what kind of person you truly are. Thank you for all the beautiful memories and adventures. I know it hasn't been easy, but it's so worth it. I can't imagine my life without you, and I'm so glad you chose me to be your wife. Thank you for giving me the two most precious gifts in the world.

To Chloe and Safiya, Mommy loves you so much. Being your

mother is my greatest joy. You have always motivated and inspired me to work hard and keep trying. I am truly amazed at all of your talents and beauty. Thank you for helping me every day. I hope you know how much I love you and always will.

Thank you to Heavenly Father for hearing and answering my first prayer.

—CAROL

I hardly know where to begin. I wish I could say I sat down with Carol and this book just flowed like water, but that is far from the truth. So many people helped it become what it is. Thanks to the talented members of the Writeminded critique group: Liz Adair, Christine Thackery, Ann Acton, Tanya Mills, and Terry Deighton, whose comments and suggestions proved invaluable.

Thanks to everyone at Shadow Mountain, especially Chris Schoebinger, Dave Brown, Tracy Keck, and Lisa Mangum, for making the book beautiful and seeing Carol for the special person that she is.

A special thanks to Michelle Wilson, who made the phone call that changed everything. Thank you for introducing me to Carol, helping when I got stuck, being a mentor, and taking me along on your writerly adventures.

A warm, heartfelt thanks to Carol for being so willing to give of yourself and share your story in the hope that you can help others. We started as strangers, and now I'm lucky enough to consider you a dear friend.

Thanks to my parents, Lynn and Julene Parsons, who, when I told them I was going to write a book, never doubted I could do it. They just waited for me to finish and encouraged me while wearing matching shirts and smiling faces. Thanks to my children, Madilyn, Emma, Garrett, and Grant, who bring laughter and joy to my home.

To my husband, Jeremy, the deep thanks that can only go to the one who saw all the highs and lows as I tried to find the right words. Thank you for your love and support. You're my Best.

And finally, thank you to my Heavenly Father, from whom all goodness flows, for knowing what I could do even when I didn't.

—STACEY

Bibliography

Angelou, Maya. Facebook post. July 4, 2011. https://www.facebook .com/MayaAngelou/posts/10150251846629796.

Caussé, Gérald. "We Are the Architects of Our Own Happiness," CES Devotional, November 4, 2012.

Frankl, Viktor E. *Man's Search for Meaning*. New York: Pocket Books, 1984.

Haight, David B. "Love All," *Ensign*, November 1982.

Keller, Helen. *The Story of My Life*. Cutchogue, NY: Buccaneer Books, 1976.

Moltmann, Jürgen. *Theology of Hope*. London: SCM Press, 1967.

Nazarian, Vera. *The Perpetual Calendar of Inspiration*. Highgate Center, VT: Norilana Books, 2010.

Osbon, Diane K. *Reflections on the Art of Living: A Joseph Campbell Companion*. New York: HarperCollins Publishers, 1991.

Tolkien, J. R. R. *The Lord of the Rings*. New York: HarperCollins Publishers, 1994.